Finding Her Way

A Woman's Journey

Sydney J. Reuben

Copyright © 2009 by Sydney J. Reuben

Growling Tiger Publishing
P.O. Box 50516
Palo Alto, CA 94303-0516

Cover Design by John Axtell
sixaxseven@gmail.com

Cover Photo by Emily Hallowell
ehallowell@yahoo.com

Book Layout and Graphics by Cynthia Ng
www.cyngraphics.com

Author's Photo by Suzanne Peck
suzanimals@msn.com

ISBN 978-0-615-27133-0

Library of Congress Control Number: 2009901862

This book is lovingly dedicated
To the two women who did the most to shape me and show me what unconditional love is, Mom and Aunt Sophie. To the two women who honed me and continue to lovingly accompany me on my way, my daughters Robin Reuben and Beth Breslin. And to my two muses, who prodded me to begin writing this book and inspired me all the way through, Growling Tiger and Crouching Little Girl.

Better fly, Butterfly,
now is the time.

Contents

Note: Poems are indicated in italics

Expression

Expansion

A Different Kind of Book

One day at a friend's home, when agonizing about getting nowhere with the self-esteem book I had been trying to write for years, my friend said something so bizarre that I didn't think of it again for a very long time. She said, "Sydney, you should write your autobiography." In total astonishment I replied, "I'm not famous and I haven't done anything extraordinary. Why would anyone want to read it?"

It was several years until I received an answer to my question. I was about to read one of my poems at a women's group. Because of the poem's brevity and my nervousness, I chatted with the women for a couple of minutes about what was going on in my life at the time I'd written the poem. That personal commentary had a surprising effect: It seemed to bring the poem off the written page and make it more real for the listeners. So every time I recited a poem after that, I added a personal anecdote. Both the poems and the commentaries were always received with heartfelt appreciation by those with similar experiences. At last I knew why people would want to read about my life—because the stories are theirs as well as mine. However, I did not write an autobiography, as my friend had suggested. The subject of this book is not me but the journey, a woman's journey to finding (and re-finding with each of life's transitions) her sense of self and her right way of being in the world. If you're a woman reading this book, chances are that much of it might be part of your journey as well.

Finding Her Way is a different kind of book in that it uses several literary formats. As well as the poetry and commentaries, there are also fairy tales, anecdotes, and vignettes (really short stories), all depicting the journey away from a life fractured by fear, repression, and self-judgment toward one of freedom, empowerment, and unconditional self-acceptance. I had no plan to write a slightly different book about the journey. It just came out that way.

It is my fervent wish that you will treat this book as a loving friend, for that's how it was written. I hope you will take time with it, too, reflecting on each piece before going on to another. Very possibly the writings will evoke something in you. It might be an emotion, a memory, an insight or an opinion, similar to mine or the polar opposite. Whatever it is, I invite you to write it down, either in prose or in verse, in a notebook or a journal. The questions at the end of each segment were designed to help you express your experiences. Of course, you can read the book straight through without answering the questions; but if I've enticed you to pick up pen and paper, I wish you as much joy with your writing as I have had with mine.

I can also envision this book being read in women's circles and book clubs, with group members having the fortunate opportunity to share their adventures in an accepting environment. Why? I have found that once our stories have been heard and validated by others, we are better able see that they are, after all, merely stories. Then we are better able to let go of them and embrace a more present, free and expansive way of being in the world.

There's one last thing I would like you to know about this book: Because it's not an autobiography, the individual pieces have not been arranged in chronological order but by topics. As you read along, you will find the story goes back in time, then forward, then back again with a different or even the same theme. And isn't that how life goes?

Expectations

Take One

Knock, knock. (I open the door.)
"Hi, Sad Sydney, how nice to see you."
Sad Sydney feels acknowledged and
smiles, despite her depressed mood.
I slam the door in her face.
Sad Sydney feels rejected and even sadder.

1 The Invisibility Cloak

She Didn't Have Blonde Hair

The little girl took one tentative step into the room and froze. It was like no room she'd ever seen. There was one corner devoted just to puzzles. Another had a life-like fort with a door for kids to go inside and play. Beneath the towering windows, the entire length of the wall was filled with books on shelves low enough that she could actually reach them. But what captivated her most was the kitchen. It looked like a *real* one, with a stove and refrigerator that were almost as tall as she was, and all sorts of dishes and pots—just like her mother's kitchen.

Her mother was now encouraging her, "Go on, honey. It will be alright. You can play with the other children and have lots of fun."

But it was the other children that kept her frozen. So many were blonde-haired and blue-eyed. Seated at the tables in the center of the room in their fresh-looking clothes, they seemed to have walked right out of one of the picture books behind them. The little girl could almost see grains of sugar from gingerbread cookies powdering their red lips and cheeks. And they were all staring at her. Their blonde hair glowed like haloes around their heads, and their blue eyes looked at her in a way she had never been looked at before. The little girl had no way of knowing that the prolonged stare was the last 20 seconds they would give her.

She leaned back, into her mother's belly, as if trying to return to the safe place she'd once inhabited. "It will be alright," her mother soothed again. "Come on, dear," and taking her quivering hand, walked the little girl to the small chair at the table where the teacher indicated she should sit. And then her mother left her among all those strangers. She just left.

At some point, the teacher told the class it was play time, and everyone dashed to one area of the room or another. By the time the little girl caught on to what was happening and scooted over to the kitchen, the four girls who were there had already assigned roles and told her there was no part left for her in their make-believe household. Always having played with her older brother, she'd had no idea how bossy little girls could be. Her stomach felt queasy and she tightly squeezed her eyes shut. "No, no, no!" she thought. "I can't let them see me cry."

Keeping her eyes to the floor, she made her way to the fort where several boys were loudly playing. Usually her brother included her, especially if a parent told him to. But there was no parent here and the teacher, already immersed in a book, was oblivious to her plight. The boys went right on playing as if she weren't there.

Using every bit of her will to hold back the tears, she sidled over to a lone boy seated at a table. "Can I work the puzzle with you?" her high, thin, little girl's voice pleaded. "No," he mumbled without looking up.

She took down another puzzle and sat at a table by herself. She somehow managed to fit together the tear-moistened pieces and make it through the longest, most painful half-day of her life.

When her mother came to collect her, she ran up and melted into her legs. "How did it go?" came her mother's always-cheerful voice. And taking the most courageous step she was capable of—one that would become a lifelong habit—she swallowed deeply and said, "It was alright."

To Be Seen Without Being Seen

Almost 60 years later, I was not surprised to find myself the oldest member of the 20-person training program. Nor was I surprised when the cliques that formed at lunch time did not include me. What did surprise me, though, was how much it bothered me, how easily my childhood wounds could be ripped open after all those years and all those tears and all my work on self-acceptance.

In my mind, I was five years old again, attending my first day at kindergarten in a neighborhood where I knew no one and no one wanted to know me. It was years later that I found out we were the only Jewish family in a parochial parish. All I knew then was that there was something horribly wrong with me. Why else would no one let me play with them? And it must have been something obvious—by just glancing at me they seemed to know I wasn't good enough.

Often I wondered why I hadn't run to my mother in tears, croaking between sobs, "No one would play with me," so she could explain that it had nothing to do with me and everything to do with bigotry. But I always knew why—I was too ashamed. My family didn't seem to see my flaw, and I wasn't about to bring it to their attention. Maybe I could pretend I was just as acceptable as other little girls and they would never find out how defective I was.

Maybe if I blended into the background, people in general wouldn't see what was wrong with me. Maybe if I were inoffensive in every way, people wouldn't notice or if they did, they wouldn't hold it against me. In short, I became invisible. I was one of those kids who showed up in class without walking through the hallways. I was just there, in the back of the room, where no one passed by on the way to their seat.

Being invisible, of course, was very lonely, but it was safe. I had no idea that I was stuffing down the pain and the sadness—and the rage. I just knew I hated that people didn't see me *even though that was my objective*. I guess I hoped that they would make the effort to notice that I really was acceptable, even lovable, after all.

Eventually, I outgrew much of my shyness and gained some social skills. I made friends, made babies, made careers, made a life. Yet, there I was after the first weekend of the training program, feeling left out, invisible, and not good enough all over again. I began to write the following poem to the sad little girl inside me, and somewhere during the writing I realized it was an ode to sad little girls everywhere.

Growling Tiger, Crouching Little Girl

My forgotten, abandoned, left out, left behind,
shunned, rejected, ridiculed, ignored, overlooked,
oh so sad little girl, you have been neglected by me.
My body seethes with your desperation.

Clenched teeth, holding back anger at all those people
who hadn't seen you, hadn't heard you,
and those who had yet discounted you.

Sore belly—is the gurgling there the growl of your anger
swallowed but not digested? A tiger of discontent?
And if I unclenched my teeth, what would you say?
"I'm here, I'm real, I feel. I think, I'm smart, I care."

My middle-aged woman can feel just as overlooked.
No longer an attractive maiden, stereotyped
as a nice, not-so-interesting older woman
by people whose lives seem far less interesting than mine.

Even some people who supposedly know me.
Why don't they hear me when I talk?
Why does it matter to me?

Growling tiger, crouching little girl, I weep for you both.
I weep for all the little girls who swallow their tiger,
whose voice, swirling in acid, churns with the unspoken rage
and unending pain of the invisible person.

The One Perfect Person

If only one person had come up to me after the event, the woman standing in front of me was without a doubt the perfect person. This had been my first public poetry reading, though I'd been writing for years. I had worked up my nerve and submitted two of my favorite pieces, been invited to read, and showed up on the appointed evening with two friends in tow, my guarantee there would be at least a smattering of applause when I read.

I hadn't felt nervous until after we arrived and I realized that most of the evening's poets belonged to writers' groups and regularly read in public. The man seated in front of me filled me in on the history of this event, as well as the writing group he'd belonged to for twelve years and various aspects of his life that I hadn't asked about. It was then that I felt like a novice and the nervousness set in.

Mr. Experience in front of me was asked to start the readings. He confidently strode to the podium, not with a couple of sheets of paper like I had in my lap but with a huge binder of his writings, sectioned off by color-coded dividers. He first warmed up the audience with some off-the-cuff quips as smoothly as Jay Leno opening the *Tonight Show*, then very calmly and expressively read three of his poems. Had I wanted to find fault with either the writing or the delivery, to somehow put myself at ease, I would not have been able to. Not only had the poems been polished to near-perfection, they were entertaining as well, the last one being laugh-out-loud funny.

Sure enough, before I even had time to think the words "What a hard act to follow," the host was announcing my name as the second reader. Knowing that my works were not of the caliber that had just been presented, I swallowed deeply and said to myself, "If my poems touch just one person tonight, I will be happy."

Then, clasping my two sheets of paper, I made my way to the podium, looked out at the small audience of writers and their friends, and read my not at all humorous poem, "Growling Tiger, Crouching Little Girl." I relaxed a bit during the second poem, which if not exactly entertaining was at least less gut-wrenching. The audience applauded politely, and I sat down to listen to the other writers.

Now, after the conclusion of the program, I faced the one person who was touched enough by my poetry to seek me out. She looked deeply into my eyes and said, "Thank you. I know what it's like to feel invisible." Then the woman returned to the side of her busily-socializing husband, Mr. Experience.

Your Turn to Pause and Reflect

Before answering the questions, please take a few moments to think or write about what the pieces evoked in you.

Questions

1. Have you ever felt invisible, or wanted to be? What were the circumstances?

2. Have you feared there was something wrong with you but didn't know what? How did you compensate for your presumed flaw?

3. Do you stuff down your feelings? Your creativity? Is there a tiger growling somewhere in your body?

4. If your little girl were to stand up out of her crouching position and your tiger were to roar, what would they say? What would they do?

5. Is there one small, courageous step you could take toward expressing your feelings and your creativity?

2 Fantasy Land

His Name Might Have Been Eddie

One evening when I was 10-ish, my dad brought a young man home from work. I think his name was Eddie. He must have been around 20, old enough to be a man, young and cute enough for me to form an instant crush.

Over dinner, there were four things I noticed about Eddie. The first was his accent. I'd been around Yiddish accents my whole life, having grandparents, aunts and uncles from the "Old Country," but had never heard such a young person speak with one before.

The second was his stammer, and the third was his hands that never stopped shaking. Why would such a cute guy seem so unsure of himself? Then Eddie (I think that was his name) laid his left arm on the table and I discovered the fourth thing. Rapt in conversation, he seemed unaware that his shirt sleeve had crept up far enough for the numbers to show. My breath caught in my throat. I tried hard not to stare, but everything else in the room had disappeared to me.

I never saw Eddie again. I don't remember anything that was said at dinner. Despite the crush, I probably forgot about him after my first game of Monopoly. But those numbers were permanently branded into my mind.

Better than Life

Given my painful rejections at school (there had been several) and now my graphic introduction to the horrors of the Holocaust (after he left that night, Dad told us that Eddie had been the only one of his family to survive the concentration camp), the outside world seemed a very hostile place. But I had already found a much more hospitable world inside my head, its usefulness was made clear to me during a family dinner.

Being the youngest in a family of six (Aunt Sophie and her son Stuart were part of our extended family, along with my brother Spencer, my parents and me), everyone seemed to do everything faster than I did. Especially eating. Most often by the time I finished my first helping, there were no seconds left. I eventually learned to gobble my food as the rest did, not so much to get another helping but to avoid being left out of the game or other family activity that followed dinner.

However, it wasn't my slow eating that drove my mom crazy, it was my pokiness in getting to the dinner table. I was often playing or doing something else right around dinner time. This particular evening, I needed to use the bathroom. I suppose this must have happened many times before because my usually even-tempered mom blew her stack and said, "If you like it so much in the bathroom, you can go right back and eat your dinner there!"

Stunned, I meekly took my dinner plate and fork into the bathroom and sat down on the closed toilet, feeling banished and ostracized and completely powerless. I later learned that no one expected me to last in there for more than a few minutes, just long enough to learn my lesson. But I stubbornly stayed there throughout dinner and fantasized about being so big and powerful that nobody could tell me what to do.

When I finally emerged, I pretended that the punishment hadn't bothered me. I did learn to be more mindful of time, but I also learned something much more empowering: There was a place inside my mind that I could escape to when life was too hurtful for me. Over the years, I lived in my special place to a continually greater extent.

In my imagination, no one could harm me and anything, except disappointment, was possible.

The Three Sisters

Once upon a time in a nondescript town, three maiden sisters lived together in what had once been their parents' modest home. They worked hard in the town's department store for their meager salaries and lived simply. Their looks, their interests, their lifestyles, everything about them was unexceptional, except for one thing—they all had wonderfully vivid imaginations. When each sister was alone in her bedroom and let her mind play, she was transformed into a different person. The youngest sister became a prima ballerina, the middle sister a brilliant doctor, and the oldest a concert pianist.

Five days a week, the three sisters were on their feet all day long, waiting on customers who were often indecisive or demanding. After work, the sisters prepared dinner and did household chores before dragging their aching feet to their bedrooms. But once their minds began to wander from the mundane, the youngest sister exchanged her support hose for imaginary dance tights, the middle sister switched from calculating bills to making uncanny medical diagnoses, and the oldest sister's no-longer arthritic hands effortlessly played Chopin before a swooning audience. No matter how trying or tedious their day had been, the sisters always had something wonderful to look forward to at night, something which never failed to put them on top of the world.

Then one day, some strangers came to town. "Just passing through," they said. There was much whispering among the townspeople who had heard from friends in neighboring villages about some odd-looking travelers who had magical powers. Before they left town, the strangers were caught shoplifting by the sisters, who dutifully informed the store manager, who dutifully notified the sheriff, who dutifully made the arrest. In a burst of passionate vengeance, the strangers placed a curse on the three sisters, wishing for them the worst thing that could possibly happen.

Poof! The youngest sister was a prima ballerina, the middle sister a brilliant doctor, and the oldest a concert pianist.

An Unlikely Prince

With the help of my wonderfully vivid imagination, I made it through grade school and junior high. Subsequent to being the new kid in kindergarten, there were a few more family moves with painful adjustments. Occasionally, I found myself part of the "in group," but mostly I hovered on its fringes. Always, I felt not good enough and had my alternate fantasy world to escape to. In high school, I watched a lot of TV and played cards with my family. Mom urged me to get out more so I could meet people: "Do you think Prince Charming is going to ride up on his white horse and ring our doorbell?"

Ironically, that's pretty much what happened. Because he played bridge (brilliantly for someone who was only 19) with my cousin Stuart, my prince-to-be spent a lot of time at our house. He was very cute, treated me kindly and, of course, I had a crush on him. One evening he came over (in his brown car, not on a white steed) and rang our doorbell. When I told him Stuart wasn't home, he asked me out. I was flabbergasted! Could dreams really come true?

We were married a couple of years later. It seemed like I was living out my fantasy, but I was on very shaky ground. Like the romantic movies at the time, my fantasies had always ended with the happy couple declaring their love for one another. I had no concept of what went on after that. I also had no understanding of emotions, no ability to appropriately express them, no experience in (nor role models for) joint problem-solving (didn't you just try to force your preferences on the other person?), and no inkling of what true intimacy was all about.

Unfortunately, those deficiencies were among the few things we had in common and the marriage was doomed from the start. As I grew progressively more miserable, I lived more and more in Fantasy Land. It got to where that world seemed more real than the "real" world. I remember one crucial moment when I knew I had to choose between permanently crossing over into my alternative world (becoming certifiably insane) or remaining in the world of loneliness and disappointment. Had it not been for my two young daughters,

I don't know what my decision might have been. I wound up choosing the fence: I would not leave my daughters, but I would not completely abandon my alternate world, either. As before my marriage, I continued to fantasize about meeting Mr. Wonderful.

The Metaphysics of Anticipation

Can you miss someone you haven't yet met?

Can you remember a voice you've never heard
and listen for a familiar word
from someone with no name or face?

Can a tune bring nostalgia for what hasn't occurred,
triggering tender memories blurred
from a future time and place?

Like the tree in the woods falling to the ground,
does someone not yet met make a sound?
Get lonely? Impatient? Think of me, too?

Can you miss someone you haven't yet met?
Well, I do.

Your Turn to Pause and Reflect

Before answering the questions, please take a few moments to think
or write about what the pieces evoked in you.

Questions

1. Have you experienced a personal holocaust that scarred you
    in some way?

2. How have the effects of that scarring shown up in your life?

3. What do you do to escape from the "real" world?

4. What did you learn from your role models about emotions
    and communication?

5. Did you learn anything when you were growing up that
    prepared you for intimate relationships and/or marriage?

3 Stereotypes & Shadows

I Was Well Fed

I've often wondered why I hadn't bonded more fully with my mother in childhood. I think it had a lot to do with traditional gender roles. Mom was the one who cooked and cleaned and made sure the children were fed, clothed, and in good health. She didn't play with us—that was part of Dad's role, as well as going to work and making the bigger decisions. He was the head honcho. Mom was more like the maid.

On the week days when the others were at work or at school, Mom would put on a stack of platters (the large, breakable records also called "78's") to occupy me while she did her housework. I would sit on the couch, rocking rhythmically, back and forth, back and forth, to Liszt, Tchaikovsky, and Rimsky-Korsakov. Their names sounded so exotic. Their music took me to other dimensions.

Every half hour or so, Mom would reappear and flip the stack of records so the reverse side would play. At some point, lunch would be provided. It was an efficient system. The composers babysat me so Mom could get her work done. I blissed out on classical music, was safe and well fed. I don't remember us interacting much, except when Mom had all her pre-dinner work done and before my brother and cousin came home from school. Then it was time for Mom to relax with her *Redbook*, a popular women's magazine (in those days that meant recipes, romantic stories, and articles about how to be a good wife and mother).

Mom would lie on her stomach on the bed, reading the soap opera type stories, and I would brush her hair. Usually, the brushing felt so good that she would fall asleep. For me, it was my one chance to play with my mom—well, her hair—and to let my creativity soar. In my mind, I was designing fabulous coiffures as I twisted the hairbrush this way and that.

One day I decided to make particularly large curls by twisting the brush round and round, picturing how full and gorgeous they would be. I kept turning the brush while Mom peacefully dozed.

She awoke to find the hairbrush hopelessly entangled in her hair. "What did you do?!" she asked/accused. That evening, my aunt cut the brush out of Mom's hair. I remember it took a long time for the hair to grow back. I don't remember ever again playing with her hair or any other part of Mom during my childhood. The composers continued to babysit me, Mom still got her housework done, and I was always well fed.

Something else had happened, though. At age four, I knew that I didn't want to live the life my role model was living and began emulating her less and less.

I Did What Was Expected of Me

Our family's biggest concern was that I would grow taller than my brother, who was older than me by three years. While he was learning his Bar Mitzvah service standing on a stool to be seen over the podium, I was learning to slouch to be *not* seen over him *anywhere*.

It was way before the Women's Liberation Movement and strict gender roles were still the norm. Women habitually went into one of three careers where they supported their male managers: nursing, teaching, and office work. But mostly they did what was expected of them—they got married and raised families as their "real" profession. I remember my brother telling me men were better than women at everything, even the "womanly arts." When I mentioned cooking, he said the world's best chefs were male. When I countered with sewing, he counter-countered with such names as Oleg Cassini and Christian Dior. Like most people in our culture, it never dawned on me that the reason men were at the top of every field was because of the differential way boys and girls were raised. And to rub salt in the collective woman's wound, society had a pejorative expression for women who really wanted to get married and have a family. It was called going to college to get an M.R.S.

I was not one of those women. As a child I had dreamed of having an exciting career, like investigative reporting. But after several years of cultural indoctrination, helped along by Mom telling me that boys wouldn't like me if they knew I was smarter than they were, my childhood fantasies fell by the wayside in adolescence. Still, I never dreamed, as did most teenaged girls I knew, of a husband and a suburban home with two children, a dog, and two cars, one of which was a station wagon for driving carpools. Yet that, in fact, was my life by my late 20s. I had been properly acculturated.

The marriage never had a honeymoon period. I was no longer in love with my husband before we even got married, but I was too young and insecure to say anything to anyone. I thought I was being "realistic," that people couldn't go around being in love their whole lives, that they settled into a comfortable routine with one another. Only, I was never very comfortable. Something inside—my creativity, my sense of adventure, my Self—kept yearning to escape.

Probably the most disempowering aspect of being raised in a patriarchal society, for me, was not having my own identity. Mainly, women were known by the men in their lives. And when we married, we lost not only our maiden name but our first name as well. It was usually with great pride that the former Mary Jones would read envelopes addressed to Mr. & Mrs. John Smith. Again, I was not one of those women. I just did what was expected of me.

The Silent Scream

It was one of those nights that I dreaded. I had dutifully dressed to impress the wives of the men my husband wanted to impress at "the country club." I don't know about other country clubs, but this one was a place where people of humble beginnings showed off their *nouveau riche* finery to one another. Being more *nouveau* than *riche*, we frequented the club only occasionally, as guests of my husband's business associates who could afford the steep membership fee. I had always hated going there and had no inkling I was about to experience a life-defining moment.

The people at our table were in the midst of the usual conversation, in which the men spoke about business and sports while the women talked about the only things that were sure to be inoffensive enough to not embarrass their husbands—recipes, fashions, and vacations.

The moment happened in the middle of our discussion about whether the current season's hemlines were one or one-and-one-half inches above the knee, which was right after the conversation about the "in" vacation spots where Americans could go to exotic-sounding islands and stay at American-owned hotels with every conceivable American convenience. I was thinking that this seemed like the identical conversation we'd had about 20 times before, when suddenly I saw these women. I mean I *really* saw them—perfectly coiffed, expensively dressed and bejeweled, talking about things that had absolutely no meaning for me. I was aghast. They were the Stepford wives—and I was one of them.

After nearly ten years of trying to be what I thought was expected of me as the wife of an up-and-coming businessman, I no longer recognized the me I had become. My fake smile maintained a façade of composure while inwardly my soul emitted a long, blood-curdling, "NOOOOOOOO!!!!!!!"

Claiming the Bed

The cat seemed to know before we did that my husband and I would soon be parting and wasted no time proclaiming himself the alpha male of the bedroom. I imagine he had formulated his strategy over several years of observing my husband sprawled over three-fourths of the bed, snoring loudly, spittle slipping out of the corner of his mouth onto the pillow beneath.

During those years, the cat had merely hunched his back after we'd gotten into bed and jumped sideways on tippy-toes, glaring steadily at my husband. This time, though, he boldly leaped onto the bed and began wedging himself between the two of us. He made me laugh.

Weeks later when my husband left, the cat somehow knew he was gone for good and not merely on one of his business trips. Now each night after I got into bed, he walked slowly toward me in a stalking mode, purring loudly, eyes fixed on me, drool slithering down his fur. He made me nauseous.

It reached the point of "Oh, my god, we have got to get rid of this cat!" the day he peed around the bed. My daughter had been showing signs of a cat allergy for months. Suddenly, I began itching and sneezing, too.

I didn't spend days working up my nerve to ask him for a divorce, as I had with my husband. I just found the cat a good home. And there I was, alone in my very own bedroom, for the first time in my 28 years. I felt no need to map out my territory as the cat had, nor did I sprawl over it as had my husband. I simply climbed into the bed—*my* bed.

Finding Her Way

From Under His Shadow

He was my daddy, and I adored him.
He was very smart and very playful.
But when he was depressed, he was very depressed.
And when he was angry, he was *very* angry—
the heavens and the ground shook.
I listened for the first rumblings and made myself small.
Daddy's little girl.

He was my brother, and I adored him.
He was so charming and comical,
everything was more fun when he was around.
Everyone else thought so, too.
And I was an afterthought, an also-ran,
my brother's little sister.

He was my knight in shining armor,
smart like my daddy and charming like my brother.
There was a time when I adored him, too,
before he reserved his charm only for others.
And I became the dutiful wife, the smiling hostess,
the "little woman."

He was my first date after the divorce.
He was very charming, also—I wasn't his wife.
Then he looked at me and said,
"Now tell me about *you*; I hear your ex-husband …"
So I took back my maiden name and moved to California,
where no one knew my daddy, or my brother, or my ex-husband.
And I could be bigger than his shadow.

Your Turn to Pause and Reflect

Before answering the questions, please take a few moments to think or write about what the pieces evoked in you.

Questions

1. Do you keep yourself smaller than you could be? In what ways?

2. What sort of role model was your mother (father, for those men reading this)?

3. Which familial or societal expectations did you/do you find most limiting?

4. What expectations do you put on yourself? In what ways do they restrict you?

5. If you were to be bigger than anyone's shadow—your own, society's, or another person's—what might your life be like?

4 Taking Off

On the Brink

Click, click, click. Each cog slowly fits into place as the roller coaster creeps up the enormous first hill.

There's such promise, so much potential with fledgling ideas, would-be ventures. Does the real ever live up to the imagined? At what point does possible turn to probable and probable to actual? And does actual necessarily become eventual old hat?

Click, click, click. With each cog, my heart beats faster in anticipation of the tremendous rush soon to come.

A new place to live. So many arrangements to make, cartons to unpack, furnishings to buy. And when the final accessory is hung on the wall, how long will I enjoy it before my eyes become so accustomed to the sight that I no longer see it?

Click, click, click. Almost to the top. The excitement borders on panic.

A new job, with mountains of information to absorb and new skills to acquire. How does an uncomfortably steep learning curve morph into satisfying mastery, then to "been there, done that"?

Click, click, click. Tottering at the top and looking down. The anticipation is almost unbearable. Is it too late to get off?

The meeting of someone new, so full of unknowns and differences. Must excitement vanish when strange becomes same? Must same become same old? Is old necessarily dull?

Click, click, click. How does one stay on the brink, that place of endless possibilities?

No Way Out but Out

I was wound so tight I felt like the least thing might cause me to explode, not emotionally, but really explode into a thousand pieces. Mom couldn't help but notice and offered to stay with the girls so I could get away for a few days.

Being fairly new to the Bay Area and not knowing the environs well, I hopped in the car with no plan beyond heading north, up the coast. I drove through San Francisco, shoulders so taut a good jolt might cause them to snap. Into Marin County, nothing had changed, but I'd discovered my radio wouldn't work. No person, no music, no anything to block out the thoughts in my head.

I kept driving and driving, with no human interactions, even when I stopped for gas or food. Except for the few hours that I slept in a motel, I kept heading north in a futile attempt to drive away from myself. Amazingly ridiculous, but with hindsight I believe that's what I wanted to do—drive away from my extremely uncomfortable self.

I wound up somewhere in Oregon a day or so later and stopped for a stretch break. Walking alongside Hwy. 1 without my glasses, I struggled to make out something on the ground about 20 feet ahead of me. I slowly walked toward what looked like lots of little lines on the pavement, each about 2-3 inches long, packed into a very small area. Squinting as I edged closer and closer, suddenly there was a big WHOOSH and a splash of color so magnificent my jaw almost hit the highway.

Having always been a city gal, I was unaccustomed to observing the natural world. I had no idea that a flock of gloriously-colored monarch butterflies would look like a pack of little lines when they were at rest. When I got to the motel that evening I realized that those butterflies had shown me what was bothering me: I had been living in the Bay Area for almost a year, spending considerably more time dreaming than doing. I felt stuck, and frustrated, and did I mention STUCK?

Better Fly, Butterfly

Better fly, Butterfly, now is the time.
    Your wings are closed
    so no one knows
    the vibrant colors you hide.

Better fly, Butterfly, now is the time.
    Waiting's a net,
    don't let it get you
    caught up inside.

Better fly, Butterfly, now is the time.
    To spread your wings
    and do all those things
    you've never even tried.

Better fly, Butterfly, *now* is the time.
    Or else you may
    find that "someday,"
    somehow, just never arrived.

Time to Get Moving

Most of my life, I had played it safe. From doing what was expected of me, to trying to be invisible, to playing whatever role seemed to be called for—I was anything but a risk taker.

Getting divorced was my first big risk. Moving to California was my second. It was time for me to spread my wings and crash if need be, but I could no longer let fear of failure and rejection keep me and my life small. It was time to get off the brink and do the exploring I hadn't done before I was married.

The Serendipity Trail

Once upon a time, two young cars were about to set out on their maiden journey of life. Dale knew exactly where he was going—San Francisco, with all her beauty and opportunity. "Why don't you come with me, Ollie? I'm taking the direct route which will get me there in a couple of days."

"No, thank you, Dale," replied the second little car. "I'm just not sure yet where I want to go or what I want to do. I think I'll take the Serendipity Trail and let her lead my way."

"Well," shrugged Dale, "if you ever get to San Francisco, give me a honk." And off he went, making every planned stop at the designated hour and reaching his objective right on schedule. It was a tiring trip, but he had lots of enthusiasm for making his fortune in the big city.

Ollie wasn't quite sure when he wanted to leave, so he hung around for a while until one morning the sun smiled at him so brightly he knew it was the right day. He washed and shined himself, threw his belongings into his trunk, and took off at a leisurely pace down the nicest looking road he could find. He stayed on the highway for quite some distance until a narrower, winding road beckoned him. Following the signs of Serendipity, Ollie took the new road, enjoying for several miles the interesting twists and turns.

Then suddenly Ollie saw smoke and heard screams. He screeched to a stop in front of a tumbled-down shanty that was in flames. A man ran up to him, yelling that his wife was hurt and needed help. Ollie flung open his doors for them to get in, then floored his gas pedal until they reached the hospital. He nervously drove back and forth in the parking lot for what seemed like hours. Finally, the man appeared with a big grin on his face.

"I don't have no money, but I'd sure like to thank you for saving my wife's life. I don't know what we'da done if you hadn't happened along. Not many cars travel that road, you know … too winding to make good time." Ollie's paint had been scorched a little by the fire and his upholstery had absorbed a lot of smoke, but he beamed with pride as the man thanked him.

Ollie decided to keep on the road until some other branch of Serendipity beckoned to him. However, all the twists and bumps of the country road were loosening his bolts and jumbling his plugs. He was very tired, but wanted to make it to the top of the large hill in front of him before stopping for the night. The grade was steeper than he had anticipated and he had to struggle to keep going up the hill. He gave it all the energy he could muster, keeping his pedal in passing gear. When he finally lunged to the crest and began his rapid descent, he saw a herd of sheep crossing the road at the bottom of the hill.

Ollie couldn't stop in time and swerved to miss them. He rolled over, smashing one of his windows, and came to a halt in a muddy ditch. Two shepherds ran over to Ollie and after several exhausting tries, pushed him out of the ditch. "Gosh, we're sorry, but there just isn't any other place for our sheep to cross," one said. "Let us make it up to you by putting you up for the night."

Sore and tuckered out, Ollie was grateful for the invitation. He fell asleep as soon as they showed him where to park and slept soundly the entire night. The following morning, the shepherds filled him with gas and washed off the mud as best they could, but when Ollie went to let them inside he realized he'd lost a door handle in the accident.

Ollie went back up the hill to look for the handle just when the sun began to rise. He had been so tired and scared the night before, he hadn't taken a look at the valley below. It was incredibly beautiful. He stared for several awe-filled minutes, without moving, without thinking, without making a sound. He inhaled the beauty of the silent dawn, feeling a perfect oneness with the world. He never found his missing handle, but he didn't care. He felt more energized and better-calibrated than if he'd had the most thorough tune-up money could buy.

Now Ollie was feeling loose and ready to resume his trip. He drove with all his windows rolled down, allowing the world to come in and the loving feelings he had for the people and the countryside to go out. He followed the Serendipity Trail for several months,

Finding Her Way

accumulating many experiences, many friends, and lots of feelings he'd never known about.

Ollie eventually made it to San Francisco and was able to locate Dale. Filled with excitement to see his old friend from home, he drove up honking all the way. "Egads, Ollie, is that you?" cried Dale, recognizing the sound of his friend's horn more than his appearance. "Stay away from me until you get cleaned up—you're a mess! I knew you shouldn't have taken that crazy route. I couldn't even find it on the map."

Dale was highly polished and sleek looking, quite the San Francisco sophisticate. "Where have you been? I got here in three days and have been realizing all of my dreams. I started as an independent cab, and now I manage a whole fleet of limousines! But look at you. Your window's smashed, you're missing a door handle, your paint is scorched, and you smell awful. If you'll pardon the pun, Ollie, I think you've become a bit shiftless. What have you got to show for yourself?"

Dale's paint had been buffed to such a high sheen that Ollie was able to see his own reflection. Dale was right—he looked like a mess. Plus, he had no job prospects and he still didn't know where he was going.

After a quick clean-up, Dale took Ollie to a fancy service station for lunch and told him of his plans to expand. "I know you'll want to come with me this time, Ollie. There's no stopping us. As long as we follow my plan, we can get everything we ever dreamed of."

Ollie, enjoying the luxury but feeling a little woozy from the unaccustomed high octane level, thanked Dale for his hospitality. "I appreciate the offer, Dale, I really do. But there's an ever-so-exciting lady waiting for me who's got adventures and wisdom you and I couldn't even guess at."

"Well, bring her with, Ollie. I've got a fiancée, too."

"Sorry, Dale, maybe I'll see you both someday—on the Serendipity Trail."

Your Turn to Pause and Reflect

Before answering the questions, please take a few moments to think or write about what the pieces evoked in you.

Questions

1. Have you ever been so uncomfortable that you wanted to run (or drive) away from yourself?

2. Do you prefer to plan your experiences or let Serendipity lead the way?

3. What roads have fear of failure, disappointment, or other repercussions kept you from traveling on?

4. What vibrant colors are you not showing? What would you look like as a butterfly with its wings spread?

5. What in your life are you dreaming about or on the brink with right now? Can you take just a little risk with it?

Finding Her Way

Exploration

Take Two

Knock, knock. (I open the door.)
"Hi, Sad Sydney, how nice to see you."
Sad Sydney smiles, despite her depressed mood.
"Please come in and make yourself comfortable."
Sad Sydney begins to relax,
feeling acknowledged and allowed.
"Okay, it's time for you to go now."
Sad Sydney's face falls.
She feels sad, rejected—and tricked.

5 A Checkered Career

From Expectation to Exploration

When I began journeying on the Serendipity Trail, after so many lack-luster years of traveling on expected routes, life became a series of explorations in four main areas: careers, relationships, personal development, and life's truths. Although I struggled quite a bit with each, I was compelled to keep trudging on. There was no turning back because there was no safe place to return to.

My search for truth would eventually lead me to my haven within, not the fantasy world of my mind but a bottomless treasure trove of what I value most in life. The journey has been quite circuitous, as I kept looking for life's jewels outwardly. And though I never would have guessed it at the time, much of the impetus for my forward motion had been provided by Miss Kangas in our 7th grade English class. She showed me how to walk away from what no longer fits.

Thank You, Miss Kangas

Her stint at our junior high school lasted only a couple of months. I suspect that was the duration of her entire teaching career. She might have entered the field of education with the hope of imparting some bit of wisdom that would guide her students through life. If that were the case, and unless she's still alive and by some magnificent miracle happens to read this book, she'll never know that her dream was realized—at least for this student.

At that time, 7th graders were the most difficult students to teach; perhaps they still are. Tottering between childhood and adolescence, we often represented the worst of each stage. Ironically, I fit in with this class of misfits better than any other throughout my educational history. I found I had a propensity for throwing both spit balls and sarcastic barbs and, in general, acting almost as obnoxiously as our class's best smartasses.

Miss Kangas tried, with what seemed her maximum capability, to teach us English. Every day she tried. Every day our behavior was incorrigible. Every day she wound up in tears. We twelve-year-olds were far too busy bowing to peer pressure to be compassionate.

Once a week or so, she made an impassioned plea. She did not beseech us to behave better, nor even to do our homework. Instead, she implored us to never work at a job we did not enjoy because we would be doing it for eight hours a day—more time than we would spend doing anything else in life. The first time she said that, I mentally sat bolt upright. The thought that working would take up more time than anything else in my life was both astonishing and appalling. *Who would want to do that?* And if it were true, why was our teacher working at a job that consistently caused her to cry?

Then one day, I was surprisingly sad to see a man standing at the head of the room when I walked into our English class. He told us he was substituting for our former teacher who had left unexpectedly. We students cheered for our victory (we had succeeded in getting rid of one of "them"), but a part of me was cheering for Miss Kangas. She had heeded her own words, and in a rare moment of moving beyond my almost-adolescent-total-self-absorption, I sincerely hoped she would find a job that did not upset her so much.

Now as I think of it, perhaps Miss K is better off not knowing that it was nothing she'd told us about English but her words of extreme frustration that have guided me throughout my multi-faceted working life. Eight hours a day is, indeed, too much time to spend doing something I don't enjoy.

Hopscotch, Anyone?

Looking for my right livelihood kept me job hopping. In fact, until my late 50s, I had never worked in any one place for more than two years. Every job was fun for me at first because I loved to learn and was able to quickly pick up new things. New information, new processes, new strategies, were all fascinating to me—at first.

After the initial steep learning curve and mastery of skills, I became bored. Then Miss K's internalized voice would haunt me, "You're spending more hours at work, Sydney, doing something you no longer enjoy, than you spend doing anything else in life." And like my 7th grade role model, I was out of there.

My career exploration included a few extended periods (i.e., more than two years) of self-employment mixed among my various jobs. Here I heeded Joseph Campbell's advice to follow my bliss. The money that followed was enough to get by, but not enough to enable me to quit scrambling and after a few years, I was back in the job market again.

I've worked in administrative support, management, marketing, sales, weight control, hypnotherapy, life coaching, workshop presentation, group facilitation, self-esteem counseling, editing, résumé writing, and job interview training (I'd been on so many interviews, I declared myself something of an expert).

Like Goldilocks, I kept trying this job and that, but none of them fit "just right" for very long. In time I came to realize that this leg of my journey was not so much about careers as it was an exploration into self-identity. I had moved away from the influences of family and the conservative Midwest. Now it was time to learn who I was as an independent adult.

A Relative Perspective

Did I spend sleepless nights worrying about not having a steady income? Yes, frequently. Did I wonder what was wrong with me because I didn't seem able to stick with something for very long? Yes, sometimes. Did I share friends' concerns that I would become a bag lady? Well, once in a while.

Then one day while speaking with my cousin Stuart about his possible retirement in a few years, I got a whole new slant on my situation. Stuart had been the only one of our generation of cousins who had become a "professional." (That meant a doctor, lawyer, dentist or CPA.) He became an attorney at a time when that profession was still admired and built a long, distinguished career.

I had grown up with the assumption that when someone was a "professional," they were set for life: no job security worries, no money worries, no career worries at all. That's why I was surprised by the plaintive note in my successful cousin's voice when he said, "But I don't know what I would do if I retired. I've only been an attorney. I don't know how to do anything else."

Did I say I was "surprised"? *Floored* is more like it. I don't remember what my verbal response was, but inwardly I grew about 5 inches. I was no longer a misfit who couldn't hold down a job. I was someone with a 30-year history of being gainfully employed in various fields. I was someone whose career kit overflowed with tools. I was someone who knew she could always get a job, quickly learn new skills, and make a real contribution to whatever organization employed her.

I wasn't a fuck-up after all. I was a multi-talented, highly employable woman!

Match Game, Perhaps?

One day Aunt Sophie (Cousin Stuart's mother), who was character-istically sweet and upbeat with a kind word for almost everyone, was acting in a very uncharacteristic way. We were discussing relatives, as we usually did on her yearly visit to California, when a distant cousin's name came up and Sophie began criticizing him for being dour and caustic.

I was trying to be nonjudgmental of others and didn't want to play the "Let's Trash the Cousin" game. Merely blurting that out would probably seem like a chastisement or, even worse, a holier-than-thou-ment. What to do?

The two things I knew about this cousin were that he had a sharp mind and a dull job that he probably didn't enjoy for even one hour a day. My mind put it all together and came up with an all-too-common picture of a miserable man, full of frustration, who took it out on others.

Then I was struck with a flash of creativity. "Sophie," I said with excitement in my voice. "How about playing a game?" To my always-playful aunt, this was like asking a child if she'd like to eat cake and ice cream for dinner, and Sophie immediately said, "Sure, what game?"

"Oh," I replied, "let's call it the "Right Career Match" game. For instance, that cousin you were just talking about seems to have an astute mind that he's not able to utilize at work. If neither age nor education were a factor, what profession do you think would suit him better?"

"Hmmm," she began, "maybe a lawyer or even a judge." she said, clearly getting into this new game.

"Yes!" I shot back, just as eagerly. "I can see him in that profession, using his mind in a more constructive way. Now, what about my dad?" (A product of the Depression Era and not having finished high school, Dad had never found his right career match, either.) "Sophie, I probably never mentioned to you that on my first day in a university classroom, I thought, 'I can see my dad up there in front of the class.' What do you think? With his love of learning and clear way of explaining things, wouldn't Dad have made a great college professor?" She readily agreed.

"Now, Sophie, what about you?" (She had been a bookkeeper for most of her working life, and neither numbers nor attention to details came easily for my ADHD aunt.) "Without consideration for education or training, what do you think would have been your right career match?"

She deliberated briefly and said—in a complete turnabout from her usual self-deprecating manner—"I think I would have made a good nurse."

"Sophie, that's exactly what I was thinking!" I exclaimed. We then enjoyed some lovely bonding moments discussing our shared vision of her in a spiffy nurse's outfit, putting her nurturing talents and love of helping others to good use.

The next day, I mused over an important difference between Aunt Sophie and Cousin Caustic. While neither had found their best career match, Sophie was almost always happy and, in her 80s at that time, "took it out on others" by walking two miles, twice a week, to volunteer at the VA hospital while on her vacation. With or without a job title, Sophie knew who she was and how she wanted to be in the world.

Hello, I'm Sydney

Hello, I'm Sydney. I'm a life coach who helps people make meaningful changes in their lives. And I'm also an editor and a workshop presenter.
No, those are titles of jobs that come and go.
That's not who I <u>am</u>.

Hello, I'm a caring and compassionate mother of two, grandmother of six, and friend to many.
No, those are other roles that come and go.
That's not who I <u>am</u>.

Hello, I'm a woman who loves to read, hike, play puzzles and games, and sing in a barbershop quartet.
No, those are interests that come and go.
That's not who I <u>am</u>.

Hello, I'm a woman who is dedicated to her inner growth, striving to be consistently authentic, to do her best with whatever life brings her, to learn from her experiences and become ever more conscious.
No, those are desires and intentions that come and go.
That's not who I <u>am</u>.

Hello, I'm a kaleidoscope of thoughts, feelings, desires, and sensations that change even more frequently than my job titles.

Following the Sisters

Despite my growing insight about the relationship between career and identity, I continued to hopscotch along, all the way to age 58. At that time, I was simultaneously engaged in three completely different careers—résumé writing, independent clothing sales, and self-esteem counseling—to be able to pay the bills and keep from being bored with any one of them. Just when I was despairing that there was no right career match for me, one that would be enjoyable, meaningful, *and* financially viable, Serendipity called in her sister, Synchronicity, to help show me the way.

It happened like this: After working on my own for several years, one Saturday morning I woke up knowing that it was time for me to get a part-time job, which would allow me to continue to do the self-esteem work that was so satisfying for me while supplying some guaranteed income. I also knew it was important to work in a place that had a family feel to it—I'd grown tired of both living and working alone.

All that day, Serendipity nagged me to pick up a particular local newspaper, but I had a lot of résumé work to finish and couldn't get away. By the time I made it to our town's main shopping area, it was late afternoon and the bins that had earlier held the local newspapers were now empty. I went from one corner to another, unable to locate a single paper.

Returning to my parked car, I walked by a row of shops. As I passed in front of the cleaners, Synchronicity, in the form of an Asian woman with a camera in her hand, popped out and asked if I would take a picture of her and a friend. "Sure," I said, and snapped a couple of shots. *Here comes the good part:* As I handed the camera back to the woman, I spied on her counter what I imagined was the last newspaper left in the entire town. She gladly gave it to me in appreciation of my "camera work."

As you've probably guessed, the newspaper contained an ad for the exact job I had in mind: a part-time administrative assistant to the interim Academic Dean at a nearby graduate school. How wonderfully temporary it sounded! What's more, the school was known for its humanistic values and emphasis on community. The ad had my name written all over it, and by Wednesday the job was mine. *Here comes the really synchronistic part:* I found out in the interview that the Saturday newspaper I'd been pushed all day to find was the final issue in which the ad had run. The two sisters, Serendipity and Synchronicity, had done their job well.

But the story is just beginning. From the start, the school felt like home and after just one month, I asked Human Resources if there were a full-time position that would take advantage of some of my other skills. I was told there might be something opening up in a few weeks.

In the meantime, one of my job duties was to take minutes at the faculty meetings. I recognized that my role was to be a fly on the wall, speaking only if I needed help in following the discussion. But at one of the meetings, Synchronicity was in attendance. The faculty had just agreed on the need for a final editing check of the doctoral students' dissertations before they were ready for the Academic Dean's signature. The Dean's question, "Who has time to do this?" was met with a faculty chorus of "Not me!" Then, as if acting with a will of its own and with Synchronicity's full encouragement, slowly my hand began to rise. What was I doing, a brand-new, part-time administrative assistant, offering to edit doctoral dissertations? Before I could rethink my offer, the Dissertation Director had given me eleven 200-page, scholarly tomes to check!

Ah, the two sisters work in ways I am rarely able to guess in advance—that's what makes them so exciting. It turned out that none of the doctoral candidates knew anything about this newly-instituted final check. They thought their exhaustive work had been completed. Suddenly the rules had changed, and I, someone they didn't even know, was the person who had to inform them. Yes, it bordered on ugly. As well as using every bit of diplomacy I could muster to avoid being stoned by the irate students, I called upon my training skills to teach them the writing technicalities they needed to know. Most of the students wound up being very appreciative.

Here comes the best part: One of those students worked for the school as an Admissions Counselor (I hadn't even known such a profession existed). Because she had been impressed with how I'd handled the delicate dissertation situation, when the student graduated and resigned from the Admissions Office a few weeks later, she recommended me for her position. My willy-nilly, multiple-careers journey had given me the "just right" background for this job: one-on-one counseling, small group facilitation, sales, and administration.

It was a career match made in heaven. At last I'd found something I enjoyed doing eight hours a day. Soon, the days became weeks and the weeks became months and, lickety-split, my first year flew by. Several more months passed and my Pavlovian conditioning kicked in. When the two-year bell rang, I began salivating for change, itching for a new road to travel on.

But this time I didn't leave. Thirty years of job hopping had shown me I could fend for myself. It had also given me a sense of self tied to neither a title nor a job description. However, there was something important that I had not yet learned: how to work collaboratively with others. And what better place to learn that than at an institution where people actually listened to one another when they talked? I finally was ready to commit, and now have been working in the same place for several years.

However, I had been playing another game of hopscotch over the same 30-year period since my divorce. Could I also commit to a personal relationship? First, I had to find the right match.

Your Turn to Explore

Before answering the questions, please take a few moments to think or write about what the pieces evoked in you.

Questions

1. Did you have a teacher who taught you something that made a real difference in your life?

2. Have you found your right livelihood? What makes it so?

3. If you haven't yet found it, and if neither age nor education were a factor, what would be your right career match?

4. How has your relationship to your work mirrored your personal relationships?

5. In what way is/was your identity tied to a job title or other role? Who are you without any role at all?

6 The Dating Game

Yesterday's Newspaper

Strewn across the sofa,
front page crumpled, coupons rent,
blotched with coagulated jelly,
it looks soiled, ravaged, spent.

Slowly Dow Jones starts to move
as beneath, a dully aching head
dares a peek at the sun
through a slightly puffy eyelid.

Gingerly she rises,
a yawn ghoulishly distorts
mascara streaks
replacing last night's rouge.

And pushes from her eyes
once-bouncy curls
now limply hanging,
exposing their dark roots.

Moaning, she bends
to retrieve her pantyhose,
all rolled up,
one little foot pro-
trudes.

She showers and powders,
she dresses and combs.
Plum makeup creates shadows,
erase-stick covers her own.

Gulping toast and coffee,
head pounding appreciably less,
she unfolds today's edition
of tomorrow morning's mess.

Dating, the Great Escape

I have been single a very long time—my whole adult life minus the ten years I was married. And being that the number one pastime for a single woman (at least when I was younger) is looking for a romantic partner, that amounts to a whole lot of dating. Although I was never quite the party girl described in the previous poem, I spent a lot of time looking for love in a lot of wrong places. Rather than being an exciting exploration, trying to get to know a total stranger (aka, dating) often amounted to a distraction or an avoidance of getting to know myself.

Oddly enough, one of my least noteworthy dates has stayed with me all these years. It was with a newly-divorced man who was in the bemoaning stage of grieving for a marriage he must have thought more wonderful than his wife had. Maybe it "became" better after he was no longer in it. At the beginning of the date, during the obligatory exchange of life histories, he referred to the time spent with people who mean nothing to him as collecting "un-memories." I loved the term so much that I optimistically thought this date might become a real memory for us both.

Alas, I fell more in love with the word than with its author, and the date was so forgettable I remember nothing more than that we went dancing. The expression, however, stayed with me because it and the evening sum up most of my experience with dating. After many years of exploring that scene, off and on between relationships that were few and short-lasting, I wrote this ode to dating and mentally implored my life partner-to-be to find me somehow, somewhere—anywhere but on a date.

Un-Memories

Movies with men whose names I can't place,
dinners with faces time has erased,
walks and talks capped by a forgettable kiss—
    Un-memories are made of this.

Potlucks with people I'd never met
and after the fifth time, we hadn't met yet.
T.G.I.F. parties and round-robin tennis—
    Un-memories are made of this.

Swinging in the park with John, or was it James?
Dancing my feet off with ... they all seem the same.
They all blend together and none do I miss—
    Un-memories are made of this.

My Queendom for a Word

What is the word for the state of being single? There is no noun like "partnership" or "relationship," only a much maligned adjective. It's hard to think of "single" without associating it with words of dissatisfaction, like "lonely"; or insufficiency, as in lacking a partner; or something temporary and without much substance, as being between relationships.

Given that I've spent considerably more time "between," my exploration of being single has been much more extensive than that of being part of a couple. Over the years, I've become quite comfortable with myself and my life and, therefore, would like to suggest some new words for referring to a more positive state of being single.

Singlehood: the status of belonging to a desirable group, like when one is a member of a sisterhood or a knighthood, or simply "the hood." Singlehood requires esoteric knowledge of the group's ways and confers upon its members a sixth sense that allows them to recognize one another at a glance.

Singleship: an attained way of being, similar to statesmanship or craftsmanship, that implies a level of mastery. Singleship skills include enjoying one's own company, the ability to make one's own decisions, and taking full responsibility for making one's way in life.

Singledom: the domain over which a single person rules, including her living space that she can decorate anyway she wants; her possessions that cost whatever amount of money she deems acceptable; and her activities, opinions, and food, all of which she chooses without needing to confer with anyone else.

I think these are wonderful words, empowering words, representing a state in which one can take pride. I hereby proudly announce my singlehood. It is no more temporary than any other state of being. It has not been foisted upon me, but freely chosen, at least for now, because I honor that way of life. Furthermore, I possess the requisite skills for singleship and the confidence needed to successfully reign over my singledom.

Your Turn to Explore

Before answering the questions, please take a few moments to think or write about what the pieces evoked in you.

Questions

1. Did you/do you take pride in your singlehood, as a free choice, or do you see it as an undesirable state that was thrust upon you?

2. Did dating ever seem like something you did to avoid being with yourself?

3. What have you learned about yourself from dating?

4. What function did/does dating serve in your life in addition to an opportunity to meet someone who could be the right fit?

5. Do you have some funny (now that they're over) un-memories? Some scary ones?

7 Romantic Relationships

First Love

It was love at first sight. He looked at me with undisguised eagerness. I looked at him with eyes that threatened to grow larger than my small head. My heart pounded so hard my whole body trembled. His backside visibly shook with anticipation. I ran to him, threw my arms around his neck, and buried my face in his fur.

I was an eight-year-old girl on our family's annual car trip to Florida to visit my grandmother. He was a full-grown collie, the most gorgeous dog I'd ever seen. I wanted to believe he was Lassie, despite my brother's sarcasm about the screen star being tied to a pole in the yard of the motel that we'd stopped at overnight.

I begged to be allowed to stay with him, but my parents insisted I eat dinner with the family. The next morning, I could hardly wait to run outside to play with him again. Afterward, I waved goodbye through the half-cracked car window, my heart fully broken. At every subsequent motel stop on every subsequent trip, for the next few years, I looked for him. It was not to be.

I'd had my first big lesson in love: Relationships last as long as they last (meaning, there's no way to extend their shelf life past the point that my head and my gut tell me it's over—even though my heart doesn't want to hear it). It would be many years before I actually *learned* that lesson. And many more before I learned my second big lesson, that love, like matter, is neither created nor destroyed.

Relationships, the Other Great Escape?

When it came to relationships, I seemed once again to be 18 years old—the age I'd been when I married—as if I'd been in an emotional and social state of suspended animation for ten years. I had a repertoire of only three modes: 1) gaga in love, 2) struggling to keep the gaga in love state alive, and 3) despair when it was apparent that resuscitation was impossible. While in the third and final relationship mode, I never ceased to be amazed at how many tears my body could produce. Each time, I was sure I would never love that way again. And that was true, I never did love quite the same way again. But the heart has truly wondrous recuperative powers and after many months of healing, I was right back trying it again.

I usually could tell by the second date if I both liked and was attracted to the other person. Most of the time it was two-dates-and-out. On those rare occasions when I fell in love and saw the person long enough to call what we were doing a relationship, I most often found myself on an emotional roller coaster ride. The highs and lows were exhausting and although my heart felt crushed when the relationships ended, the rest of me was glad to get back on my solid single ground.

At times I was a dating machine, trying to convince five-year-old Sydney that she was good enough. If I could get someone to fall in love with me, that meant I was lovable, right? It would be embarrassing to tell you how many years it took me to find out the answer to that question, so I won't stop to calculate. But I will tell you my answer: It just meant that I'd become somewhat talented at periodically getting someone to fall in love with me.

The first time I had genuine feelings for someone I was dating and he genuinely cared for me was a momentous occasion. Unfortunately, I didn't realize it until after the relationship ended. We'd been so comfortable and joyous together that it came as a complete surprise when he told me he loved me but wanted to find someone more suitable for his lifestyle. I was devastated. In between pleading and crying, I aimlessly walked around my neighborhood, staring at the trees uncomprehendingly. *But I love him and he loves me. Why isn't that enough?*

I Don't Know When

I don't know when
you became the sparkle in my day,
the laughter in my life.

I don't know when
you became the comfort in my pain,
the joy in my sorrow.

Alas, I don't know when
you became the chill in my dreams,
the fear in my love.

But I know precisely when
you pulled away from me—
life became colorless.

Close, but No Cigar

It took three more loving relationships spread over 20 years, with much more time spent getting over the breakup than being together, to learn why mutually caring for one another isn't enough for a healthy relationship. During that period of time, I'd started exploring two of the things that I needed to learn: unconditional self-acceptance and honest communication.

Although my romances were not teaching me those important relationship skills, I was learning some very valuable lessons. I learned, for instance, that my discomfort about falling in love with someone a lot younger than me came from myself and had little or nothing to do with other people who I thought were judging us. I learned that the attraction to people who are quite different from me is very exciting at first, but that similarities are important for the long haul. I learned that my partner becomes more physically attractive to me in direct proportion to the deepness of my feelings. Most important—although it took a while—I learned to relax and enjoy my romances. In fact, there were times when we'd had so much fun, I found that most of the wet spots in bed were from my tears of laughter.

And there was even a time, when I'd felt our bodies were in the way of our getting as close physically as I was feeling emotionally, that something happened which still mystifies me. Suddenly, my partner and I were both without bodies, suspended somewhere in space, clearly in a different dimension. It was one of the most amazing experiences of my life (second only to childbirth). Yet, there we were the next day, playing our control games again as if that astounding shared experience of oneness hadn't occurred.

Although all four of my mutually loving relationships produced many *real*, very beautiful memories, the fit was never quite right. I have yet to experience an extended period of intimacy with a romantic partner, the kind that will deepen over time more than my age lines.

The Dance of Intimacy

Come closer she invited.
I'll come as close as is
comfortable I replied.

Come closer she implored.
I'm as close as I want to be
for now said I.

You're withholding and
distancing she accused.
I took a step backward, confused.

You haven't been honest
she blamed.
I walked away.

Stuff 'til You Bust

It's true that I always seemed to attract someone who wasn't quite right for me, but it's also true that I wasn't quite right for intimacy. With so many "real" things in the world to be concerned about, it's astonishing how many molehills I can enlarge, distort, and make into monsters.

Growing up in a household somewhat like a '50s TV family, where saying the word "damn" or getting divorced were thought of as a disgrace and unpleasant feelings were something that didn't exist until they periodically roiled to the surface and exploded, I didn't have a clue what to do with my uncomfortable feelings but to stuff them.

That meant I had to smoke, drink, or overeat. "Skinny is beautiful" was the slogan of the day, so that made overeating quite a handicap. Drinking more than a small amount of alcohol made me sick. That left smoking, which I began doing at an early age. (People had not yet grasped the correlation between tobacco and lung cancer.) But when I was only 26, taking my first tennis lesson, the instructor made me stop halfway through because I was so out of breath and red in the face. She was afraid I might have a heart attack.

I quit smoking, yet for the most part, I was still successful in stuffing my unpleasant molehills. Except, sometimes they burst out in strange ways and scared the hell (I mean heck) out of me, and I developed various physical symptoms from so much holding in. But perhaps the most unfortunate consequence was that many of my tender, loving feelings were stuffed, too, beneath my defensive armor.

I Am a Beautiful Artichoke Heart

I am a beautiful artichoke heart.
It's quite pleasant basking in the Watsonville sun,
showered by morning mist, cooled by evening breezes.
Ouch! An insect bit me. Okay, it's not always pleasant.
Oh no, here's another one. Owww!
I'm so exposed, Mr. Moon, I wish I had something to protect me.

ح

Hmm, it's not so bright this morning,
like a cloud has hidden Mother Sun.
And there's a nasty bug coming at me. Oh, I can't look.
Wow! That bug hit one of these green flaps and bounced right off.
Flaps? That's why it's so dark. And I probably don't look like me.
But who cares as long as they keep the creeps away?
Everyone knows I'm a beautiful artichoke heart.

Look! Here comes that big bully crow.
Wait until he tries to peck at me.
Eek! He's going to pluck my flaps right off.
He's going to get to my heart-self and devour me.
Oh, help! Somebody do something.
He went away! Squawked like hell, then flew away.
Ho, ho, it must be these prickles on my flaps.
Talk about ug-ly! But they sure do the job.
And everyone knows I'm really a beautiful artichoke heart.

ح

Ooo, here comes Señor Farmer—what a dude!
He makes my prickles tingle and my flaps flutter.
He's the one I've kept my beautiful heart-self intact for.
And he's reaching for me!

I can hardly breathe I'm pounding so.

Señor is jumping up and down with his finger in his mouth.

Wait! Don't go. It's me, really.

I, I am a beautiful artichoke heart … honest.

I <u>am</u>. I really am. Really … I am … honest.

Life Partner—to Be or Not to Be

I have wanted a life partner (well, off and on) for so long that I'm beginning to wonder if the term means it will take a lifetime to find my partner. Even though we've yet to meet, I feel like I have made significant progress toward being a person who is capable of the partnership I want to be part of. Similar to my experience with careers, I gradually developed a sense of self that's independent of whether or not there is one special relationship in my life. I know I could continue to be happily single; yet, there are times when Serendipity whispers to me and shows me glimpses of a possible partnership somewhere down her trail.

As might be expected, just as I have changed a great deal over the course of this journey, so has my imagined partner-to-be. For one thing, somewhere along the path, looking for Mr. Wonderful became looking for *Ms.* Wonderful. Go figure! This shift felt like a natural evolution: As my appreciation for myself grew, so did my appreciation for other women. Or was it the other way around?

The focus seemed to shift, as well, from how the other person would treat me—adore me, pamper me, help me feel good about myself and my life—to what the relationship would be like—mutually respectful, based on shared values and goals, cemented together with compassionate and honest communication, and overflowing with fun and lots of other yummy things.

Often I wondered if the person I wanted for a partner were really the person I wanted to *be*. I still don't have the answer to that question, although I seem to become more like her every day.

Looking for Wonder Woman

No, she's not an Amazon who
stops bullets with her metal bracelets,
but the woman of my dreams is
quite a wonder.

She's gained strength from experiencing
the depth of her sorrow and
found that life's slings and arrows
pale by comparison.

So, too, has she experienced
the depth of her love, and
knows that moments of perfect union
are worth working and risking for.

Her kindness toward others
is an extension of her self-love.
She gives with abandon
for the sheer pleasure of it.

Mature as full-bodied wine,
she delights in her womanhood,
her sensuality, her Mother's nature,
her sweetness and warmth.

She's playfully serious
and smiles through her tears.
She's so filled with wonder,
she's wonder-full.

And I wonder where she is.

I've Only Just Begun

I am amazed and greatly appreciative of how far my journey has taken me, from that scared little girl who couldn't tell her mother how hurt she felt to this woman that I am today, who at times actually cries in front of others without a whole lot of shame.

I know that there is so much more to experience beyond my ordinary single existence. There have been events, similar to the joint out-of-body experience, when the energy of two people clicked into perfect alignment, catapulting us into other realities where the whole was much, much greater than the sum of our parts.

Yet, it feels like I've only scratched the surface in my exploration of relationship and intimacy. I can imagine permanently breaking through the defensive walls that separate me and others to where the exceptional becomes the ordinary, the extraordinary becomes the norm—all without losing one bit of the magic.

Your Turn to Explore

Before answering the questions, please take a few moments to think or write about what the pieces evoked in you.

Questions

1. If you are/were happily single, what about partnership has been appealing enough for you to want to give up your singlehood?

2. Do you have a sense of self that remains constant or do you get "lost" in your intimate relationships?

3. Describe the person of your dreams. How is that person similar to you and how does that person differ?

4. What things are important for your partnership to succeed? What are you actually committing to in a "committed" relationship?

5. Are you the person who is capable of those things? Are you currently living them rather than wanting them from someone else?

8 Real Relationships

The Move to California

"Maybe today you'll make a friend and feel more comfortable," I said to Robin, my shy first-born. She nodded half-heartedly, more in acknowledgement than in agreement. "Have a good day, honey," I added.

Robin left the car and slowly walked toward the middle school that still was foreign to her after a month of classes. Things like outdoor hallways and lunch tables speckled with pigeon poop seemed absurd to my twelve-year-old, whose entire school experience prior to our moving to the West Coast had been inside Michigan's brick buildings.

I watched until Robin disappeared through the school's doorway. Then I cried, as I had each of the previous 29 days. I tried to sound cheerful and optimistic when speaking with her, but my heart broke every time I watched my gentle daughter's diminutive form walking, so ill-equipped, into the battle of being the new kid in class.

Beth, my nine-year-old, had been just as adamant as Robin about not wanting to leave her friends in Michigan. And on the evening before her first day at the new school, she'd whined about not knowing anyone in her class. Yet, it came as no surprise to Robin and me that our precocious Beth made friends on the very first day and that after the first week, seemed to be the most popular kid in fourth grade. But Robin, as I had been at her age, was too self-conscious to be popular.

The same questions went through my mind as they had the day before, and the weeks before that: Had I been overly selfish to insist on moving thousands of miles from friends and family to start my new life? Had my mother secretly cried after she'd left me in kindergarten that first day? Might Robin never make a friend and be forever miserable?

As it happened, Robin did make a friend that day, another new girl in the class, but it took a few years for her to develop a circle of friends. "Families are uprooted everyday because of fathers' job opportunities," I periodically reminded myself. But I wasn't her father, and I had no job opportunities, and guilt was an emotion that just wouldn't quit.

My Best Relationship Teachers

As exciting as they'd been, my romances had taught me surprisingly little about being real with others, and most of what I now know came from my other intimate relationships—those with close family and friends, who unintentionally became the white rats in my relationship laboratory. And, as often is the way with experiments, there were many trials and some odious side effects.

The Worst Thing I've Ever Done

I like to blame it on our family's communication pattern, but my conscience has never let me get away with that. Growing up, the only direct communications about something unpleasant occurred when we children did something "wrong" and were scolded for it. Otherwise, anything that bothered us about someone, especially if we were afraid it would hurt their feelings, was told to a third party. Experience assured us that it would get passed on from one person to the next and eventually be told to the person it was meant for. However, each person put their own spin on the message and the originator could only guess at what the final iteration was.

Yes, I know it's very dysfunctional, but that was the communication system I grew up with. As a result, I got to adulthood without knowing how to speak directly to another person about something that bothered me. And, yes, it was one of the reasons I was so unprepared for marriage or any other close relationship.

At the time of the disastrous event, I was 34, divorced, and eager to move to Northern California to start my new life. My brother and his family had moved to Southern California a couple of years earlier. Mom was a widow living with Aunt Sophie, and I felt guilty about being Mom's second child to move so far away. During my brother's visit, I talked to him about the situation, hoping he'd tell me something that would dissolve the guilt. I cannot remember the exact conversation, but based on the outcome I must have said something like, "I would invite Mom to come with, but I know she wouldn't leave Sophie." When Spencer talked to Mom, instead of explaining (for me) why I was moving to California, he must have said something like "Sydney would like you to move with her and help with the two girls but didn't think you would." Mom must have heard "My daughter and granddaughters need me." And she did the one thing I never expected her to do—she left Sophie to live on her own for the first time in my aunt's almost 70 years. I was shocked, both for Sophie and for myself. I had only said something about inviting Mom because I was sure she wouldn't accept. Living with my mother was not how I'd imagined my new life to be.

Now that I'd gotten into this situation, though, there didn't seem to be any way to get out.

Mom moved to California with us. She settled into her new/old familial role of the mother, cooking and cleaning, and doing various other domestic chores she hadn't done much of for many years. The best things about the arrangement were that it gave Mom a new adventure, my daughters two parent figures, and me more time alone with Mom than I'd ever had. Enough time to appreciate what a loving, giving, open-minded woman my role model was.

The not-so-good thing was that I discovered Mom and I had little to talk about that was of interest to us both, other than the girls. After a couple of years, I discovered the worst thing about our arrangement: While Mom was playing the mother role, I had taken on the father role of working, making the big decisions—and not being home with my daughters after school. Mom was the one they were talking to about how their day had gone and by the time I got home, they had no desire to tell the story all over again. I felt an unintentional wedge growing between my daughters and me. Also, I thought it was time for them to start learning how to take care of themselves and contribute to the running of our household, now that they were both teenagers.

I didn't know what to do. Mom had made a life for herself in California, including a new set of friends and a part-time office job. She was thriving, and the girls loved having two parents again. But I was becoming more miserable by the day. I spoke with a couple of friends about my situation. One of them, someone I considered very intuitive and wise, said, "Sydney, you want the impossible. You want to ask your mother to leave without feeling guilty. That's not going to happen. Yet, you still need to do what you believe is right."

It took me several days to work up my nerve to talk to Mom, but a lifetime of dysfunctional communication had not prepared me for such a sensitive discussion. It couldn't have been worse. Having developed very little tact over the years, I blurted out that I felt I was getting farther and farther apart from my daughters, and they weren't learning to take responsibility, and I wanted her to leave. Just writing this—30 years later—I still feel like the most heartless ogre who ever lived. My mom, who had always been our emotional rock, seemed to crumble before my eyes. Despite her desperate attempts to come up with an alternate solution, I was adamant that I wanted her to return to Michigan. I write this now as if I'm talking about someone else. Had I really been that cruel? I'd tried to soften the blow by writing a story for her called "The Nice Monster," about a warm, fuzzy creature who did so many nice things for people that they became helpless and dependent. Had I really been that obtuse to think a fairy tale could heal her shattered heart?

Aunt Sophie told her new roommate she would need to leave (it's not the same as one's mother) and helped Mom pack up and move back to Michigan. They resumed their life together as if nothing had happened. My daughters and I resumed our lives together, with me as the mother and the quasi-father.

Every year, Mom and Sophie came for a visit. Over the next 15 years, I came to appreciate their strength as well as their beauty. These were not doormats for people to walk all over. These were loving women who truly enjoyed giving to others. Finally, I could begin to embrace those softer, more feminine, parts in me that I had spent a lifetime disowning.

Mom had forgiven me almost immediately, though I never actually apologized. And the whole situation was a much needed lesson for me in the importance of speaking directly and honestly to people, even if their feelings might get hurt. Yet, my friend was right—I couldn't get through it without feeling guilty. And guilt was an emotion that just wouldn't quit.

From Mothers to Daughters

The bond between mothers and daughters can be extraordinary. When the bond is strong, there's an unspoken language that they use, sometimes in gestures, at other times telepathically. For instance, I knew before Beth did when she was pregnant with two of her four children. Neither time had she been trying to get pregnant, and both times we were a continent and an ocean apart. Was it precognition or the mother-daughter direct link?

Then there was the time when Robin and I grew bored with playing a game where one had to guess what colored pegs the other was looking at. Using logic, we consistently figured it out in 4-6 guesses. To spice things up, we decided to use telepathy instead and see what happened. We then regularly needed only 1-3 guesses. Was it strictly telepathy or our mother-daughter shared mind? Or is "shared mind" what telepathy is?

In addition to that strong connection, another aspect that fascinates me about mothers and daughters is the inevitability of role reversals. I never knew when to expect them or how they would show up, but they sure did happen. Now that the reversals are almost complete, occasionally my daughters still let me play at being the mom, asking for advice they don't really need. I would like to give my opinion more often than when I am asked, but have come to realize that I can best show my daughters acceptance and respect by allowing them to learn from their own choices, and loving them no matter what.

From Daughters to Mothers

I had barely closed the door when the demanding voice practically nailed me to it.

"Where have you been? I've been worried about you!"

"I'm sorry—the meeting just ended."

"How can a meeting last this long? I've been up for over an hour wondering what could have happened to you."

She stood halfway down the stairs, in her old flannel nightgown, looking as properly admonishing as a clucking mother hen should. But that wasn't you, Mom. It was my 15-year-old daughter bawling me out.

ح

It was very difficult saying goodbye the last time you were here, Mom. The conversation on the drive to the airport was choppy and perfunctory.

"If you find my earring, would you bring it when you come to Detroit?

"Sure. ... Oh, I saw Jessie out jogging yesterday morning. She was sorry she didn't get a chance to see you during your visit."

All the while, you sat fondling your hands—a reassuring gesture of yours when you feel anxious or insecure. And I kept wondering how things would be when I visit in eight months. Will you be in good health? Will we be able to go and do and laugh and enjoy each other as we had for the past two weeks? Then I recalled how difficult it was for you and your mother to say goodbye at the end of our yearly visits to Florida.

"Don't forget," you explained to your uncomprehending children, "a year's an awfully long time to wait to see someone when you're not sure how many more they've got left."

I didn't forget, Mom. And sometimes when I glance down at my lap, I catch one hand fondling the other.

Our Townhome

I live in a beautiful townhouse in a lovely neighborhood.
The sun streams in through the glass doors,
adding its golden warmth to the kitchen.
A prism sprinkles dancing rainbows all around the room.

But they land silently,
and the glass doors slide only when I go out or in
and the neighborhood looks like an empty motion picture set
and the sun warms just my body, not my soul.

The townhouse is decorated casually in autumn colors, with
bright posters and glued jigsaw puzzles covering the walls.
An oaken wall clock and a bird-motifed light fixture
contribute natural beauty and a sense of stability.
Visitors have called the townhouse comfortable and friendly.

But only people or animals are friendly,
and the glass birds don't sing
and the clock's chimes seem to scream,
and the fall colors look drab when I'm alone.

The Empty Nest

It might hit you all at once as your last (or only) child is walking out the door or sneak up on you, bit by bit, with each day the children are gone. It was a combination for me, perhaps accentuated by my being single.

At first, I didn't realize the nest was empty—my children were *temporarily* living elsewhere. Robin had gone away to college and I'd assumed she would return home upon graduation; but she went on living with her college friend, in an apartment instead of a dormitory. Beth was gallivanting here and there with her friends. It was only a matter of time until her money ran out and she returned home. Who knew she'd have a baby instead and the following year would be living in Ireland?

It was then that the empty nest phenomenon hit me with the full force of an avalanche, and I was pulverized. How did this happen? All those insanely hectic times when I had longed for solitude became nothing more than a "Be careful what you ask for." Where did my darling little girls go? Not only were they no longer living with me, they were no longer little. Who are these competent women that have lives so full they no longer need me? When did I sign up to do life alone?

I grappled with those questions, and the positive and negative aspects of living alone, for the next 20 years. Those years, so full of twists and turns, provided the time and space for me to make my peace with who I was and who I was becoming. Those years took me from motherhood to grandmotherhood and from maidenhood to middle age. Along the way, I had to let go of almost my entire family.

"Let's Pretend"

That was the name of a children's program with fairy tales read by actors and actresses. As a child, it was my favorite radio show. It was also my favorite game when girlfriends came over to play. We would dress up and pretend we were glamorous women or detectives or cowgirls. I loved to pretend.

So it came naturally to me, when my daughter Beth and my first grandchild Jasmine moved to Ireland to be with my son-in-law Joe, to pretend that this was a temporary separation. At least once during our weekly phone conversations I would say to Beth, "When you come home ..." and she would say, "When I move back to California ..." But after six years—and three more babies—neither of us could pretend anymore. Beth's life was in Ireland with her new family.

It took many more years and much practice for me to be able to listen with compassion to parents bemoaning their children's moving away to college (a temporary condition), to the East Coast (a mere 3,000 miles and a domestic flight away). But I was learning my second big lesson about love, that it cannot be destroyed. The part about love not being created was yet to come.

For years, it amazed me how Beth and I continued to get closer despite the miles and infrequent visits. Then one day I got off the airplane in Dublin for my bi-annual visit, expecting to run into Beth's eager arms. It was so strange. Instead, I casually said, "Hi," as if I'd seen her the day before. She casually returned my greeting as if she'd just as recently seen me. We had each become so comfortably ensconced in the other's heart that we knew nothing could ever change our love for one another.

Best Buddies

My other relationship teachers are my close friends. Periodically, I tell my best buddy that I can't imagine doing life without her. Of course, I *could*, but there's a special intimacy between close friends that I never want to be without. It's priceless beyond words to have a best buddy who loves me exactly as I am.

And the humor. I really can't imagine life without a buddy to laugh with over our dumb mistakes, my disastrous dates, her forgetfulness, and life's whimsical ways that sometimes totally befuddle us both.

Then, of course, there are the hard times. Who else would call me every single day when I'm sick, or blue—even when she's sick of being blue?

And the support, which has become essential to my well-being, is so constant that I sometimes take it for granted. Not only is my best buddy in favor of anything I want to do, she actually thinks I *can* do anything I want to do.

Sure, we get on each other's nerves every once in a while, but it doesn't last very long. We both know a good thing when we see it.

Your Turn to Explore

Before answering the questions, please take a few moments to think or write about what the pieces evoked in you.

Questions

1. Can you think of a decision you made that caused your family pain?

2. Do you still have guilt around it? If so, what is your relationship with that guilt?

3. Are you/were you fortunate enough to have a strong mother-daughter bond? If not, were you able to establish a substitute relationship with another mother or daughter figure?

4. How did you/will you make it through the empty nest period?

5. In what ways are your close friends like family? Your family like close friends?

Expression

Take Three

Knock, knock. (I open the door.)
"Hi, Sad Sydney, how nice to see you."
Sad Sydney smiles, despite her depressed mood.
"Please come in and make yourself comfortable."
Sad Sydney begins to relax and lighten up.
"Let's chat," I say. Sad Sydney snuggles in,
feeling acknowledged, allowed, and wanted.
"Have you tried writing affirmations?" I ask.
Sad Sydney feels angry, discounted, betrayed!

9 Authentic Empowerment

The Moment I Found True Power

I had just returned from a two-month retreat in the beautiful Berkshire Mountains, in Massachusetts. Imagine, if you can, eight weeks in a lush, serene environment with two workshops a day, designed for the participant to take a good look at herself and the choices she makes to be authentic and happy, or not.

Now imagine navigating through Chicago's O'Hare Airport to change planes on the return trip. Assaulted by blaring sounds and glaring lights so unlike the peaceful, rural surroundings I had just left, I found myself not wanting to re-acclimate to the frenetic energy of a large city. Then, driving home from SFO, the Bay Area seemed to have doubled its automobile population while I was gone.

It's likely that you've never given yourself the luxury of a two-month retreat (how many people have?) and might not be able to imagine how foreign and inhospitable our fast-paced world is to someone whose life had slowed down to the tempo of the trees and harmonized with the chirping of the crickets, someone who hadn't prepared a meal or written a check or driven a car for the entire summer.

Trying to hold onto what was left of my inner mellowness the next day, I drove up to Sacramento to visit my younger daughter and seven-month-old granddaughter, both of whom I had missed terribly. I had hardly entered their home and said hello when Beth, my headstrong 21-year-old, informed me that I would be babysitting for the sleeping Jasmine while she went on a job interview. She quickly finished dressing and rushed out to keep her appointment.

I found myself in a house where I knew the location of nothing, responsible for an infant to whom I would seem like a complete stranger. Jasmine soon awoke, crying her head off—even more so when I, the stranger, picked her up. Thankfully, my body's memories from raising my own little girls awoke as well, and I soon found myself balancing Jazzy on my left hip while feeding her a bottle with my right hand. In the midst of my domestic acrobatics, a cat appeared, meowing as insistently as Jazzy had cried. Juggling baby and bottle, I managed to find cat food and can opener; and by the time Beth returned, I was quite proud of myself for having successfully handled the situation.

You might guess that Beth's first words were "Thank you" or "How did it go?" or even something about her interview. Any of those guesses would be wrong. Beth's first words—laden with accusation—were "Why did you feed the cat?"

You'll need a little background information to appreciate what comes next. Beth was the quickest witted in our family and at that time in her young life, she hadn't yet learned compassion for those of us slower-witted beings. Barely out of her teens, she still enjoyed getting the better of people, mostly her older sister and me. I can see now that Robin and I enabled this by being (at that time in our lives) very emotionally reactive. By simply maintaining her Aquarian cool, Beth often succeeded in reducing us to blithering idiots.

But not this day. The two months and several thousands of dollars I had spent learning how to stay present and choose happiness were suddenly worth millions. Rather than give the knee-jerk response of defensively explaining my actions, I did not reply directly to Beth's question. Instead, I calmly observed, "I guess you didn't want me to feed the cat." Beth met my equanimity with a second accusatory thrust that previously would have thrown me totally off balance, "No, I didn't want you to feed him. I already fed him this morning!"

Did I defend myself? Did I buckle? Did I curry the favor of my usually adorable daughter? Oh, no—not this time. As if channeling a sage rather than an insecure mother afraid of displeasing her child, six sane words came out of my mouth, "How could I have known that?"

I realize that if you've never raised children or spent much time around teenagers, you might be scratching your head, wondering what was so great about that. But if you have been in similar shoes as mine, you probably recognized in an instant what a brilliant coup it was—I had given Beth no irrational ammunition that she could use against me. She was momentarily stymied. Then she said, "I guess you couldn't have," smiled, gave me a big hug, thanked me for babysitting, and told me about the interview.

Finding Her Way

On my drive back to the San Francisco Peninsula, I hardly noticed the heavy traffic. I was too enamored with feeling like a full-fledged adult.

Relearning Empowerment

That first taste of being genuinely empowered by staying present and speaking rationally, with no need for defensiveness, was so uplifting that you might think it was a quick trip for me to learn to do it all of the time. Hah! In actuality, one detour led to another and another, making for quite a meandering route back to my highway to wholeness. Having spent most of my life equating empowerment with control, I reverted to my defensive behavior of collecting "shoulds" and "shouldn'ts" with which to orchestrate my world.

Every now and then, through what seemed like divine intervention, I had an epiphany wherein I relearned the same empowerment lesson over and over again, each time absolutely sure that this was the "real deal." But between bouts of re-enlightenment, remaining centered, sane, and compassionate on a daily basis still eluded me. One hugely important aspect of authentic empowerment I was yet to understand is that I am the cause of my emotional reactions. I was still tossing that hot potato at others.

Projections, Do You *Really* Understand Them?

I was in the midst of presenting a workshop on projections, explaining that, similar to watching a motion picture, often we cannot see what's on our "film" (our inner story) until we project it onto a "screen" (usually, another person). I emphasized that projections can be a powerful tool for self-awareness if we ask "How do *I* do that?" regarding what we criticize or emotionally react to in others.

A man raised his hand and said it didn't make sense to him. "I get angry," he explained, "when people disrespect me by keeping me waiting, but I don't do that. I'm always on time for my appointments." Prompted by my intuition, I asked, "Do you ever procrastinate?" After a long pause, a startled look appeared on the man's face and I could almost see the light bulb shining above his head as he said, "Ohhhh."

He needed no more explanation, but I elucidated for the rest of the attendees that procrastination amounts to keeping ourselves waiting and after countless times of treating ourselves "disrespectfully," the one time someone else is late can become the straw that breaks our emotional back. The audience responded with ah's of appreciation.

I felt smugly wise and competent with how I'd handled the situation. Had the man been part of the "act," he couldn't have delivered his lines any better, nor me mine. Blinded by the brilliance the audience was attributing to me, I didn't see that using my understanding of projections to help others work with theirs was one way that I procrastinated in working with my own.

ح

[An example of "my own"] A corporate vice-president had hired me to whip into shape a department that had been a thorn in his side for months. The office contained nightmarishly tall piles of documents and antiquated office equipment that an untrained staff was trying to operate to process the piles of papers. It was a mess. In other words, it was this Virgo's dream challenge. I reported directly to the vice-president, who much preferred ogling his administrative assistant to dealing with mundane work. In other words, I was virtually autonomous. I worked diligently for over a year, alternately tackling one pile, problem, and project after the other until the department ran with Swiss clockwork precision.

[Enter Melanie] Someone very high up in the organization must have owed her big time, because one day she appeared on the scene, with no experience in the organization nor our operations and with the title of assistant vice-president. I suddenly had an in-my-face manager. On her first day, Melanie excitedly told me that she had lots of ideas about how to improve the department. "My department doesn't need improvement," I replied. "I've just spent a year getting it in tip-top condition." Our eyes locked and silently raged. Mine: "Back off, Godzilla." Hers: "Don't mess with me, you little twerp."

Our stand-off lasted for a few months, during which I tried everything I could think of, including taking her to lunch with the hope that getting to know each other personally would help. We shared an enjoyable conversation and vowed to support one another. That vow lasted a day or two, then once again she tried to tell me how to run *my* department. My friends all agreed that she was, indeed, a monster and that I was completely justified in feeling unfairly persecuted. When I eventually gave my two weeks' notice, the vice-president who had hired me, whose ass I had saved, who had thought I was a miracle worker, said not one word in my defense. In fact, he was nowhere to be seen and did not even say "good-bye."

ح

[Back to projections] Wouldn't you, too, agree that in the previous story I had every right to feel angry because I'd been betrayed, under-appreciated, and victimized? That is what's so tricky about projections—because my accusations were true of Melanie and the playboy V-P (yes, he was the president's son), it was difficult for me to see my own betrayal and victimization through lack of self-appreciation. I did, however, come up with this equation that helped me understand who was causing my emotional reactions:

$$\text{Kindling} \quad + \quad \text{Spark} \quad = \quad \text{Fire}$$

The Kindling is the collection of shoulds and shouldn'ts I'd been accumulating over the years that, instead of controlling my world, often wound up controlling me. (People <u>should</u> respect and appreciate me; if necessary, they <u>should</u> come to my defense; and they <u>shouldn't</u> ever criticize anything about me.)

Here's the factor that is so easy to miss: The Spark is someone being *who they are*, which is other than what my Kindling says they should be (Melanie being controlling; the V-P doing his disappearing act). The Fire, of course, is the spontaneous emotional combustion (anger, disappointment, self-pity) at the unfairness of others' treatment of me.

I was able to see that as long as the same Kindling and Sparks existed, the same emotional Fires were triggered in me—every time! I further saw that I could keep my fires burning indefinitely by continuing to add Logs (playing "Ain't It a Shame" with friends or reliving the experience in my mind). I began to bask in a much more substantial light than that of others' admiration when the bulb of self-understanding lit up over *my* head.

As my understanding continued to grow, I also noticed an extension of my projections, wherein my attitude affected others and was then reflected right back at me. We had a more sassy way of expressing that dynamic when we were kids and someone would say something mean:

I am rubber, you are glue.
Everything bounces off of me
and sticks onto you.

The Luncheon

The sprinkles started coming down harder as Kit approached the restaurant for her annual, catch-one-another-up luncheon with Mary. She began to tense, thinking about how unfair life was. Mary, whose natal silver spoon was at least platinum by now, got all the breaks while Kit, who had struggled for anything she'd gotten in life, had one disappointment after another. As she'd expected, there were no close parking spaces and after circling the block a couple of times, Kit gave up the search, took the first available spot, and half-ran for two blocks in the rain.

Feeling as limp as the salad bar looked, Kit tried to brush the raindrops from her dress and fluff up her hair as she looked around the restaurant, surprised she was the first to arrive. She quickly got a table and a glass of wine, and looked up to see Mary enter the room looking fresh, relaxed, and happy.

"Hi, sorry I'm late. What happened to you, Kit? You look like Noah left without you! But it sure is good to see you, ocean and all. How have you been?" gushed Mary. "Would you believe a car pulled out right in front just as I drove up to the restaurant?"

"Yes," sighed Kit, bracing herself for the onslaught of a year's worth of happy endings Mary would soon relate.

"… and so, what started out as a disaster wound up being a significant learning experience for all of us. My goodness!" exclaimed Mary, looking down at her watch. "I've been talking for 45 minutes. Tell me, what's been happening with you?"

Now it was Kit's turn. She condensed her chronicle into 25 minutes, ending with "… and what began as a shrewd political move ended as a financial fiasco."

And that ended their ritual for another twelve months. As usual, everything, even if not beginning as such, had ended well for Mary, while few things had gone right for Kit. After their goodbyes, Mary jumped up to pay the tab. She beamed goodwill at the hostess who, in turn, smiled broadly and wished her a very pleasant day.

Kit, gritting her teeth over the inequities of life, was unaware of the scowl on her face as she absentmindedly gazed at the hostess on her way out. The hostess merely nodded.

Giving for the Echo of It

One by one, the components of my authentic empowerment were becoming more apparent to me. Being present and communicating clearly were crucial parts. Seeing that what I reacted to in others was actually a projected self-criticism was a huge chunk. Understanding the connection between how I am being in the world and how others treat me was extremely important. Still, there was another disempowering pattern, pertaining to giving, that I had mostly ignored as one would an annoying insect. This "gnat" was a small expectation that grew into a large disappointment when I gave without receiving something in return.

I had come across the concept of doing things "for the echo of it" rather than to get something back, in a daily words-to-live-by journal. I loved the sound of the phrase, which literally echoed in my mind for years. Perhaps because I hadn't yet absorbed the message nor its importance to my empowerment.

Giving for the echo of it was one of those lovely thoughts that remained an ideal for me. I still gave—even though I didn't think I did—with the assumption that I would receive something in return, at least a thank-you. What took me quite a while to understand is the significance of *receiving*. It completes the process. Then, if the recipient turns around and gives without expectation, the echo continues.

God's Gifts

"I feel so gypped," he said, his voice full of pain and self-pity. "I gave her so much of my attention, consideration and caring, and got so little in return."

"Not so," said the Wise Woman. "You gave what you did to express your love, and she gave you the equally glorious gift of receiving it."

"Ah," he said, uncoiling his aching body from its victim's pose.

Assembling the Parts

My face always falls when I purchase an item, then find out I have to put it together. It's not the work that I object to but the instructions. To me, they are more difficult to solve than a Friday *New York Times* crossword puzzle and a #10 Sudoku put together. I want to ask the person who wrote the instructions, "What were you thinking?"

Yet, my annoyance in trying to follow the written words of someone I cannot ask questions of is nothing compared to the frustration I've had in trying to feel whole and find my right way of being in the world. There are no instructions at all; and no warranty, no help line, no consumer protection agency, and not one elected official to petition for help in figuring out how to assemble my parts.

But through all my fumbling and stumbling, I've learned two things that keep me steadfastly on my path. The first is *I cannot feel whole if I reject some of my parts.* I would be incensed if I'd worked for hours putting together a store-bought item and found that some pieces were missing—therefore, the importance of unconditional self-acceptance.

The second is that *the right way of being is individual to each person.* Lots of people have lots of advice; some people have some wisdom. All of that can be helpful, but only I can fit my parts together in a way that is right for me.

It's All About You

Before answering the questions, please take a few moments to think or write about what the pieces evoked in you.

Questions

1. Do you remember a defining incident when you handled something in a way that made you feel all grown up? How many times did you need to relearn the lesson?

2. Can you see the connection between your attitude and others' treatment of you?

3. Do you feel empowered when you give for the echo of it? Can you think of a recent example?

4. In what situations do you currently feel helpless or like a victim?

5. What "shoulds" or "shouldn'ts" have you collected that provide the kindling for your emotional reactions?

10 Self-Acceptance, at Last

When Is a Judge Not a Judge?

Answer: When it's a judge, jury, and executioner.

I don't know about yours, but that's what my judges are like. They sweep in so fast, handcuff and arrest me, deliver the sentence and have me in prison before I can croak "I object!" With hindsight, I suppose I'd started doing self-acceptance work with others so I could learn to deal with my own criticism. But at the time, I thought I had a handle on my judges; all the while they were tee-heeing and guffawing their heads off.

When they were being their most uncontrollable selves, my judges chastised me incessantly, showing no mercy. It didn't matter if I pleaded, promised, or spat in their eye. They wouldn't budge a bit. Nor did it matter what I did or how well I did it. There was always a better way or something more I should be doing.

Give Up the Judges

Maybe if I read until I'm half asleep, I can turn off the light without them haunting me. Oh, God, the click of the switch woke them up—the critics and the judges. But what's that lovely tune? No, it's just a note. Oh, it was probably my imagination.

ح

Let's see. I'm supposed to sit facing the East each morning, saying this crazy mantra over and over, and after about three months my life becomes marvelous. So-hum, so-humm, soo-hummmm, sew-hum? I'd better not forget to fix that hole in my shirt. I have so many things to do. Why do I take on so much? Then I don't do anything as well as I'd like to because I'm worrying about the other 25 things. So-hum, so-hum. Oh, look at that beautiful color! Now it's gone.

ح

I really hate these touchy-feely groupie things. I bet after sitting around telling each other how great they are, they all go home and yell at their kids for disturbing their so-humming. Wow! Feel that energy. Maybe I really am a channel. Now I don't feel it anymore. It must have been group contagion.

ح

I know I should be doing other things. I guess I'm lazy, but I want to relax and enjoy this no-thinker, just-plain-fun book. God damn it! It feels like there's a gopher in my gut. When will you leave me alone?

That's up to you.

Is death a release from your continual gnawing?

No, that's life. Death is what you're doing now.

You tease me with snatches of melodies and visions of something more beautiful.

You cut them off with your shoulds, sarcasm, and criticism.

How can I get rid of that negativity?

You must give up <u>all</u> the judges, the ones who vote "yea" as well as the ones who vote "nay."

But that's what keeps me going. One in twenty wears a white hat, tells me I'm okay.

Then you're not giving up very much, are you?"

Well, if I'm not good or bad, I'm nothing.

Just the other way around. When you judge yourself, you're only a label.

But if I don't do what I should …

You can do what you want.

But if everyone did that, things wouldn't get done. Children would be neglected, there'd be litter all around, people would take and take without thought of others … Ohhh.

Give up the judges so you can give of yourself.

Self-Acceptance, the X Factor

In mathematics, X equals an unknown quantity. On treasure maps, X marks the spot of the buried treasure. I believe self-acceptance is an incredibly important X factor, often an unknown quantity and always a portal to our internal buried treasure. And that is the core empowering piece that had eluded me my whole life. Non-acceptance was how I betrayed and victimized myself.

I doubt that even now self-acceptance is discussed in many homes, or in schools, or at social gatherings. When I was growing up, it was never mentioned—anywhere. By the time I ran into it in early adulthood, self-acceptance was a foreign concept to me. I thought I knew what self meant, the various aspects of my mind and body that I called "me," much of which I was critical. I had no idea of a spiritual me, an inner essence, the me that was as pure and beautiful as the day I was born. That jewel had been buried under multiple strata of fear, stuffed emotions, and defensiveness. And, I had a gross misconception of what acceptance meant—going along with something one doesn't like—in other words, resignation. So when my brain put the two together, the equation didn't compute:

Self + Acceptance = Being resigned to what I don't like about myself

No wonder I kept resisting it! Mostly, I resisted acceptance by judging—myself, others, situations, the world. I thought that if I accepted what I didn't like, I was stuck with it and if I wanted something to change, I needed to judge it as not okay. It took me many years to understand that I had it backwards. To complicate things further, I had no clue how judgmental I was being. When it was pointed out to me at one of the personal training weekends that used to be so popular—with the finesse of a football tackle helping his girlfriend unclasp her necklace—I was horrified.

I became obsessed with changing my behavior and from my psychology classes, I knew the first step to change was observation to better understand the current situation. What I hadn't yet learned was that a person who tends to make judgments will do it about anything she observes—including the act of judging. My working equation was now something like this:

Judgment + Awareness of Judgment = Another Judgment

I felt like I was in a huge pit of not-okayness and, wielding a very pointy spade, I kept digging my hole wider and deeper. I observed myself judging, then criticized myself for doing it, and zing! another spadeful of dirt flew out of the hole. It got to where I felt so lost in the vast pit of judgments, I feared I might never be able to climb out.

Then one day the equation computed: Self + Acceptance (real acceptance, not resignation) = Self-Acceptance. It no longer sounded like nonsense but the key to filling up the not-good-enough hole. And I knew exactly what to do. I needed to start with what was happening that moment and accept the fact that I was judging my judgments. It seemed so right, so logical, so powerful. But would it work?

That was the beginning of a 25-year career (concurrent with multiple jobs) teaching tools for unconditional self-acceptance to myself and others. I'm still filling in the hole (it was gigantic) but now the judgments I notice are fairly subtle, and over the years I've had several aha's. For instance, I learned that one of the biggest shovels I used to dig my judgmental hole is impatience. I might have complained, "I've observed and acknowledged that I was being critical, but I'm still doing it!" I now recognize that if I'm wishing something would disappear from my life (even my judging), that's not acceptance but resistance. Here's the key: Just as consistently as I have judged my thoughts, behavior, appearance, attitudes, and pace at which I progress on my journey through life—over and over and over again—that's how patiently and consistently I need to acknowledge, allow, and appreciate—over and over and over again—those aspects I previously dubbed unacceptable.

More succinctly, staying out of the pit requires accepting myself exactly as I am right now, even those aspects I initially find offensive and limiting. Then something akin to magic happens: Like a scab that is no longer needed after an abrasion heals, the undesired aspect of my personality, which wasn't my true nature to begin with, falls away by itself.

Acceptance: Easy as 1-2-3 ... 4

Take One
Knock, knock. (I open the door.)
"Hi, Sad Sydney, how nice to see you."
Sad Sydney feels acknowledged and smiles,
despite her depressed mood.
I slam the door in her face.
Sad Sydney feels rejected and even sadder.

Take Two
Knock, knock. (I open the door.)
"Hi, Sad Sydney, how nice to see you."
Sad Sydney smiles, despite her depressed mood.
"Please come in and make yourself comfortable."
Sad Sydney begins to relax, feeling acknowledged *and* allowed.
"Okay, it's time for you to go now."
Sad Sydney's face falls. She feels sad, rejected—and tricked.

Take Three
Knock, knock. (I open the door.)
"Hi, Sad Sydney, how nice to see you."
Sad Sydney smiles, despite her depressed mood.
"Please come in and make yourself comfortable."
Sad Sydney begins to relax and lighten up.
"Let's chat," I say. Sad Sydney snuggles in,
feeling acknowledged, allowed, and *wanted*.
"Have you tried writing positive affirmations?" I ask.
Sad Sydney feels angry, discounted, and betrayed!

Take Four
Knock, knock. (I open the door.)
"Hi, Sad Sydney, how nice to see you."
Sad Sydney smiles, despite her depressed mood.
"Please come in and make yourself comfortable."
Sad Sydney begins to relax and lighten up.
"Tell me all about it," I say. Sad Sydney snuggles in,
feeling acknowledged, allowed, and wanted.
"You can stay as long as you like," I say. "I love you."
I go to the kitchen to make her a cup of tea.
Sad Sydney feels really strange. What is it?
"Oh, my!" she says. "I feel truly accepted."
She quietly walks to the door, opens it and leaves.

Smoke and Mirrors, and Freedom

Somewhere along the way, I lost my blinders and was able to see that the control over my world I thought my judgments were providing was merely an illusion. This was so big for me that I think it might be for you, too, so I will repeat it in slightly different words: The control over your world that you think your judgments are giving you is only an illusion.

It's true that we have free will and can choose our intentions, our behavior, and even our emotional reactions if we're being really aware. But we cannot control others' choices and life's surprises. All the shoulds and shouldn'ts and critics and judges in the world cannot ensure safety. For that matter, all the money and power and possessions and people who care about us cannot do that either. Only the knowing that we can handle whatever life brings us can provide the security that most of us seek.

How ironic—when I began accepting that I couldn't control my life situations, I was able to see that I had been handling them all along and that my pile of kindling (shoulds and shouldn'ts) that I'd been lugging around to keep me secure was useless and unnecessary. Can you smell that sweet, fresh scent of freedom?

It's All About You

Before answering the questions, please take a few moments to think or write about what the pieces evoked in you.

Questions

1. What aspects of yourself are you not accepting? If there are many, name the ones that make you cringe inside.

2. How do you resist (judge, avoid, stuff) those aspects?

3. What are some of the things your judges say to you?

4. In what ways do you imagine your life would improve if the things you have been criticizing about yourself or others were to suddenly change for the better?

5. Can you imagine those improvements in your life right now, exactly as you (and they) are, if you merely removed the judgments?

11 Letting Go

The Library

Peter couldn't understand why there were so many delinquencies lately. He'd worked at the Library ever since he could remember and while people had always been reluctant about meeting their due dates, it seemed to be getting progressively worse. "Now, Mrs. Jones," he patiently began. "You knew when you checked out Tommy that he was just on loan. Certainly 26 years is enough time to teach him how to love and laugh and make his way in the world. There's a young lady who has been waiting her turn for quite some time now."

But people often convinced themselves that their loans were permanent gifts, being taken by surprise, then anger and grief, when their due dates arrived. More than once Peter had pleaded with his boss, "Can't we make it easier on them by giving a definite date of return at the time of check-out?"

The Head Librarian always had the same reply, "Peter, if we gave them a due date, they'd be too conscious of that deadline to let themselves become fully engrossed in their adventures."

Peter would have to go back and mollify some more. "Yes, Mr. Able, you and Sally have been together for 42 years. How wonderful for you both. The Head Librarian appreciates the loving care you've shown her and knows that you've both gained much from the experience." ... "No, Mr. Able, you can't check her out again. We regularly go through our catalogues to retire well-worn issues, and Sally is worn out. Of course, you can choose a different one. There are items all around you just begging to be picked."

But so many people wanted the same one, not understanding that once an issue has been retired, it's time for a new experience. Finally, Peter decided, with the consent of the Head Librarian, of course, to print the following list:

Library Check-Out Instructions

1. Please keep in mind that all editions come due eventually and that you're wasting valuable time if you fully appreciate them only when they are new or when you no longer have them with you. Instead, give each one your special attention every day while you still can.

2. Be prompt in returning your checked out items, as they were only given to you on loan—they do not belong to you. Clinging to them beyond their due date dulls the impact of the adventures they've given you and greatly impedes your ability to check out another item.

3. Remember that there are billions of items in the Library, each with something unique to offer you, and there are so many that seldom get chosen.

4. Do not despair. As long as you don't put yourself on the Reserved List, a hand may reach up to take you "off the shelf" at any moment.

Finding Her Way

There's No Holding On

I wrote several poems to myself about letting go—perhaps the most empowering practice of all. It's been such a difficult lesson for me. I would like to be able to give myself completely to every experience, especially a loving relationship, not keeping anything in reserve; and then let go when the "due date" arrives so that the beauty of the closeness is not tarnished by my attempts to hold onto it, by my desire to turn back time, by feeling that I've lost a part of me that can never be replaced, by closing down my heart in protection.

Sometimes I go to the ocean to watch the waves coming and going, coming and going. The beach makes futile attempts to hold onto each wave. All that happens is that some of her sand winds up in the ocean. There's no holding onto a wave that's on its way out. Yet, sometimes I try.

Oh, to Be Able to Take Back the Words

How do you tell your mother that her sweetheart of 40 years will not be coming home for dinner tonight—or ever again? They'd met when Dad was 16 and she was 14, when their widowed parents married one another and they became step-siblings. The story goes that they teased one another nonstop, until one day they realized they were in love. Probably all of us would like to think that our parents were faithful to one another; I believe mine were. And despite their ups and downs over the years, Mom always seemed to adore Dad.

My brother and I agonized in the car driving over to their place, then in the elevator, riding up to the apartment—how could we tell her? We didn't have to. She took one look at our faces and knew. She was amazing. She didn't crumble as we'd expected, nor become hysterical as I had upon hearing of Dad's death. Instead, she suffered with quiet dignity. I hadn't known the depth of Mom's strength until then.

She was only 54. That seems young to me now. She lived 23 years as a widow, never remarried, never even dated. And they were good years, active years, full years, even though I'm pretty sure she never stopped missing him. Mom didn't need to read countless books and attend workshop after workshop, as I was doing; choosing to be happy came naturally to her.

ح

How do you tell your two young daughters their father was murdered? I didn't do that, either, and I regret it to this day. I'd taken the advice of a psychologist friend. At that time the recommendation was for a trusted relative to tell the children, so that the trauma would not be associated with the surviving parent. How can a mother not be with her children at such a time? True, I was scared, confused, and angry. Yes, angry at their father (we were divorced) whom I assumed had done something stupidly reckless to have gotten himself murdered. But I still wish I had been the one to tell them, to hold them, to cry with them, to show them I would always be there for them, no matter what.

I also regret the other decision that was made—to take the girls to "view the body." The advice from the professionals was to take them to the funeral parlor so they would know their father was really dead, that he would not be returning some time in the future. Again, I listened to the "expert" advice. How horrible it must have been for my daughters to see their first dead body at such young ages (8 and 6), to see their father's skin looking like wax, the makeup grotesquely inadequate at making the corpse look peaceful.

ح

How do you tell yourself you're an orphan? How does the baby of the family become the only one left? Mom died the day after Christmas of the year I'd turned 51. She collapsed in my arms and never regained consciousness. My friends said they'd seen it coming. I hadn't. My brother followed Mom by just seven months; his 26-year-old daughter had died six weeks before him. Three of them in rapid succession—boom, Boom, BOOM! I was shell shocked for over a year. That was 15 years ago and occasionally I still grieve. I don't like being an orphan.

And the words I would like to take back? Those are the ones I had said so many times in childhood when an older person tried to show me how to do something: "I want to do it myself."

The Strange Messenger

I had heard of Mount Shasta many times during my, at that time, 17 years in California, but had never been there. Now I was visiting my friend Gabriel, who was spending the summer in that area. It was July of 1994, shortly after my mother and niece had died. I think that watching my brother, to whom I had always had an extremely close tie, bury his daughter was the most painful experience of my life—up until then.

My friend had taken me for a gentle hike on the mountain, late in the afternoon, close to dusk. We decided to meditate for about 15 minutes. I found the rock I wanted to sit on and Gabriel continued to climb, looking for her perfect spot. Just before closing my eyes, a young man paused to say a few words of greeting on his way up. Eager to meditate atop Mount Shasta, I would not have engaged him in conversation except that his Irish brogue caught my attention. With my daughter Beth and her family living in Ireland, the lovely brogue was music to my ears.

Oddly, it turned out he had never lived in Ireland but was from Amsterdam. I had heard both accents before—they sound nothing alike. We chatted for a couple of minutes and just before resuming his climb, he looked at me quite seriously and said that he'd had some other-worldly experiences on the mountain and if I opened myself up to it, I could as well. He was just about to leave when I asked his name. Frank, his name was Frank. That had been the name of my father, who had died nearly 25 years before and whose name I rarely encountered.

Inspired by this young man, who seemed to appear from out of nowhere and disappear again after he left, I turned my attention up toward the heavens, took a deep breath, and declared myself open for an extraordinary experience. Just how extraordinary it was cannot be captured in words, because the colors and the intensity of the experience are beyond my ability to describe. I think of it now as a celestial laser show, where the setting sun turned not just a portion but the entire sky incredible hues. First it was peach, then pink, then red, then gold, on and on it went for several minutes while I stood there enraptured by the heavenly glow. It filled me with feelings of awe and oneness, and a sense that all was right with the universe.

I'd never seriously considered the existence of angels before that day, but subsequent events made a believer of me. When my friend returned, I learned that she'd seen neither the light show nor the young man (her eyes had been closed in meditation). I eagerly told her about both on our trip back to the house she was renting. I hadn't been that giddy in months, nor would I be again for a couple of years.

Gabriel played back her phone messages as soon as we returned. There was no escaping the urgency in my daughter's voice imploring me to call her in two separate messages. How long could I reasonably put it off? I knew in my gut that there had been a third death in our rapidly dwindling family. I assumed it was Aunt Sophie, who had been devastated by the losses of her younger sister (my mother) and her great niece. I just didn't want to hear it, to know it was true.

I braced myself while calling Robin, yet was totally unprepared for the news. Yes, someone had died but not my aunt. It was my brother, the person I'd adored my whole life. I went berserk. I ran through the house like a maniac, screaming and thrashing for thirty or forty minutes, until I lost my voice and could scream no more, which meant I could no longer keep the news from fully entering my consciousness. Gabriel eventually calmed me with her gentle murmurings, then, exhausted, she fell asleep.

I couldn't even consider sleeping during that long, long night. My heart was crushed and my brain had all but stopped working as I wandered like a zombie through the house. Yet there was one thin lifeline that sustained me enough to function—the strange messenger on the mountain and the incredible sunset. I didn't understand it, but I felt like I was being supported from above by my dad, Frank.

I made it through the funeral week in Michigan, feeling buoyed from beneath as well as from above, like I was floating on water. When I returned to California, I was told that several of my friends had meditated and spiritually supported me during that week. I now believed both in angels and the power of distant healing. I had lost so much of what mattered to me in life, but had gained something beyond the physical world that could never be taken away.

My Personal *Titanic*

With each loss of a family member, the people around me marveled at my resiliency, as I kept meeting my daily responsibilities with apparent equanimity. I think the numbed emotional reaction we experience after trauma is akin to the disease immunity babies inherit from their mothers. Both protect us for a few months until we're strong enough to deal with life, then the immunity or numbness wears off.

I, too, had been amazed by my ability to sail along fairly normally upon my return from Michigan for the third time in seven months. That was in early August. In September, my ship hit some rough water with two events that began my emotional thawing. The first was the on-and-off-again relationship I'd been in for the previous year and a half, which became permanently off when my friend announced that his path was taking him in a different direction. By then, I'd lost most of my illusions that the relationship would self-repair and the second event, though it might seem more benign, hit me harder.

That event was my birthday, the first one in my life without my mother and brother wishing me a happy day. For so many years, theirs had been the first two birthday phone calls I'd received, their cheerful voices exuding loving wishes for me. Of course, I knew they would not be calling; but as the day wore on, the non-ringing of the phone became deafening. And through an inexplicable set of circumstances, all of my close friends forgot my birthday that year. September was also the month in which my dad had died so many years earlier. When the protective numbness wore off and the tears began, I realized I had never grieved Dad's death—I'd had two small children to raise, a bachelor's degree program that I was completing, and a divorce on the horizon.

I made it through another couple of months by greatly curtailing my activities. Then the holidays were upon me and, again, my close friends seemed to vanish. Those who usually invited me for holiday dinners were out of town that year. The rest already had plans. My sense of aloneness was so pervasive that it seemed to occupy every cell of my body. My ship hit the iceberg of a lifetime of stuffed feelings with such force that everything was sent flying, topsy-turvy. I remember being at an auto dealership to get my car fixed and bursting into tears when the parts manager told me how much it would cost.

Understanding that I was not able to carry on with my counseling practice, I got a part-time office job to help pay the bills. I also understood that I could no longer stuff my emotions—I needed to grieve. While my mind was in a muddle, life for me had become so uncomplicated and slow paced that I could see some things more clearly. I saw that the culture I'd lived in my whole life did not seem to recognize grieving as a necessary function of loving, losing, letting go, and loving again. I was astonished to realize that I had never actually seen anyone grieve. I had cleared the necessary time in my schedule and made myself available, but had no idea what to do. So I surrendered to my instincts.

Every afternoon I came home from work, ate lunch, turned off the ringer on my phone, lay down on my bed (which became my "beach") and let one wave of emotion after another sweep over me. They just kept coming, spewed out of the ocean of grief gathered over a lifetime. Did you know that emotions don't disappear when you stuff them? They seemed to have settled in my muscles, ligaments, organs—who knows where? Now they were suddenly unleashed. Not just sadness, but guilt, pain, anger, the entire emotional palette. And memories—with the release of my emotions, memories that had been stored with them came flooding out as well.

Day after day for hour after hour, one wave after another covered me with the oppressive energy of memories I thought had been permanently forgotten and feelings I'd never wanted to know. Every negative feeling in the book except for one—fear. Isn't that surprising? For the first time since kindergarten, I felt not one drop of fear, because I didn't care if I lived or died. There were times when I was so overpowered by the waves that I actually stopped breathing. My autonomic nervous system must have been overwhelmed, and I was suffocating from my own emotions. At those times, I would exhale and not feel the need to inhale. From a removed place, I observed this phenomenon with more interest than I had for anything else in my life at that time. I would quite calmly observe, wondering with curiosity rather than concern, how long my system could go without breathing. Would it actually commit suicide? I had no sense of time, but I knew my breathing was suspended for longer than I could consciously hold my breath. Much longer. Surprisingly, when my inhalations resumed, there was no gasping for air, just very slow, even-paced breathing.

The many years I had been working with self-acceptance techniques served me well. I acknowledged and allowed whatever swept over me, acknowledged and allowed, acknowledged and allowed, hour after hour, week after week. When I realized how huge my ocean of stuffed stuff was, fully draining it seemed impossible. But these were not conscious decisions that I was making; I was a robot, totally at the mercy of my emotional master.

Then one day, several months into this daily process, I experienced what Columbus must have felt when he spied a speck of land in the distance. Only it wasn't land but the tiniest bit of light at the end of the longest, darkest tunnel. Surprisingly, I experienced this distant ray as gratitude. Not gratitude *for* the drop of light—the light itself felt like gratitude. Again, it was only a speck but enough to give me a reason for living. Willingly, I tolerated hours of emotional abuse for the occasional moment of gratitude for having been a part of a loving family for over 50 years.

This period of intense grieving lasted more than a year. I never completely drained my emotional ocean; but when there was more light than muck, I left my beach/bed and rejoined the world of normal breathers. There had been few insights beyond the awareness that our society teaches us neither how to grieve nor how to support others' grieving. Mostly, people had let me be. There were a couple of friends, newer ones, who had kept in touch with me during the process, periodically reminding me that if I ever wanted to talk I could call them at any hour of the day or night. I didn't, but just knowing the offers were genuine meant the world to me. Beyond those couple of friends, no one knew what I was going through. It was the most profoundly intimate experience of my life, shared between me and me.

And I didn't need for there to be many insights because I'd had the biggest revelation I could imagine: What my multiple layers of emotions had been hiding was not a horrible demon, but joy. That must be our true nature. How amazing! All the years spent defending myself for fear that people would find my fatal flaw, and it turned out I didn't have one. Actually, I was beyond amazed.

This did not, however, lead to a permanent state of enlightenment. And you will be sorely disappointed if you were expecting that, like Buddha, I then spent weeks sitting under a bodhi tree, or even an oak; or like Eckhart Tolle, two years sitting on a park bench; or like the Peace Pilgrim, undertaking a seven-year physical and spiritual cleansing. I merely resumed my life, left the office job and did a variety of things for a few years until I arrived at the graduate school where I currently work. What changed for me—permanently—is that I no longer fear my emotions. They come and go like waves on a beach and as long as I don't hold onto them, they don't suffocate me.

At some point I decided that my former family still lives somewhere and still cares about me, but in a different, other-worldly way. Each day I give thanks to them for this wonderful life that I'm living and ask them for guidance in finding my way. It's wonderful to think that I'm not really traveling alone even though it sometimes feels that way.

My Royal Family

Once they were my entire world.
And I, the baby, was cared for, played with,
read to, taken places, occasionally punished.
And always loved and provided for.

One by one, they've all left.
My dad, king of the castle, was the first to go.
How does a castle survive the loss of its king?

The two queens (Mom and Aunt) took over
running the castle, but it had no leader,
no one to get direction and approval from.

Mom left several years later.
The heart of the castle went with her.
My brother followed soon after
and there went the laughter.

Aunt Sophie left a few years ago
with her new partner, Alzheimer's.
Only Cousin Stuart and I are left.

The castle now lives solely in my memories,
which grow fewer and dimmer each year.
An empty castle that once was.

In my heart is a new castle, where my royal
family lives. And I, the baby, am inspired,
watched over, guided, given intuitions.
And always loved and provided for.

It's All About You

Before answering the questions, please take a few moments to think or write about what the pieces evoked in you.

Questions

1. What have you learned about loving and letting go?

2. Do you know how to deeply grieve? How to support another's grieving?

3. Do you understand that some friends can "go there" with you and others can't?

4. Have you ever felt like an orphan? What is that like?

5. What does "moving on with your life" mean?

Expansion

Take Five

Knock, knock. (I open the door.)
"Hi, Happy Sydney, how nice to see you.
Please come in. Tell me, what has your
extensive search for Truth brought you?"
Happy Sydney brightens even more,
"Oh, I have discovered many jewels so far
and am uncovering more every day."
"Can you share a pearl of wisdom with me?"
"Sure thing," she replies:

> *Expect nothing;*
> *appreciate everything.*

12 Amazing Grace

The Bake Shop

Day after day, a young girl walked by the corner bake shop and peered in at the heavenly sights with longing eyes. One day the baker decided to give her the treat of her life—a key to his shop, which she could use after hours to go in and eat whatever baked goods had not been sold that day. The first evening that she unlocked the door after closing time, the young girl found herself in a sugary wonderland and scurried about taking one luscious bite after another.

When she could stuff not one more crumb into her mouth, the baker returned and asked her to name her favorites. The young girl looked around at a bunch of half-eaten pastries, pondering, "Which one had nuts all over it? And which had the super-terrific filling?" She had run around the shop so haphazardly, she couldn't keep things straight in her mind. She wasn't even sure which pastries she liked and which ones she didn't.

"Take your time tomorrow," the baker told her. "There's no hurry." But the same thing happened the following evening, and the next, and the one after that.

Reluctantly, the young girl agreed to give back the key and to be given just one pastry at a time, so she could smell, chew, taste, and digest each one all by itself. Sometimes she didn't like being locked out of the shop, and sometimes she got awfully hungry. But when she'd get just one éclair or one chocolate cupcake with sprinkles on top, she could appreciate it more fully than when there was the whole bakery to attend to at once. She adjusted.

One morsel at a time, she was getting acquainted with the baker's goods. And it was much easier this way to determine which cakes she was wild about, or which pie was the gooiest, and which bonbon bothered her belly. However, after a while she was most frequently given plain donuts—no icing, no custard, not even powdered sugar on top. After all those fancy concoctions, what a letdown! Just plain, *ordinary* donuts. She balked, "I don't want plain donuts. I want the best or nothing at all. There are plenty of other bake shops around, you know."

"I'm sad to hear you say that," replied the baker. "I love to see your face light up with delight from my pastries, but I don't have éclairs and tarts to give you very often. They cost a lot to make, and I lose money if they don't sell out that day. So mostly I make plain donuts. They're ordinary, its true, but much of the time that's all I have to give you. And while they may not be as exciting as the fancy pastries, they are just as high in quality."

The young girl pouted her way back home, and after three gloomy days she said to herself, "Yes, I could go from bake shop to bake shop, eating only the fanciest pastries, but after a while they would become ordinary, too. And, I'm so familiar with this shop, it's like home to me." She decided to try the plain donuts again, with respect for the care the baker put into everything he made.

The donuts definitely were not as sweet as what she had become accustomed to; but when she stopped thinking about what *had* been and concentrated instead on what *was*, she was able to detect subtle differences among them—this one had a touch more nutmeg, that one's shape was a bit less round. "My goodness, gracious," she exclaimed, "ordinary doesn't have to be dull. It just takes a little more looking to see the specialness!"

Finding Her Way

Appreciating What Is

I wrote the previous tale about a relationship that I was in at the time. After the initial courtship stage, I had a difficult time dialing down the intensity that I had become accustomed to. I didn't want plain donuts when I had been given yummy pastries for three months. That seemed to happen to me quite a bit. It would be skyrockets with a choir singing in the background until some mysterious time in the relationship when the other person decided to slow down and resume a more normal lifestyle. That might have been fine for them, but I was hooked! I was addicted to all the wonderful attention and compliments and falling-in-love stuff.

Just like a little girl throwing a temper tantrum, I blamed and raged and cried, rather than appreciating the wonderful few months we'd shared. And perhaps we would have been able to enjoy more time together had I eased up on my expectations. After so many years of working to escape parental and cultural expectations, there I was putting my own onto others.

It took me a few repeats of this story—different people, different settings, but basically the same story—before I stopped being angry at the other person for pulling back and started realizing that it was, once again, my attitude that was making me suffer.

I haven't fallen in love in many years, and sometimes I wonder if my fancy pastry days are over for good. With slightly high cholesterol levels, I haven't even had plain donuts in ages. They sound great! But what's even greater is my growing appreciation of what I have while I have it.

Doctor Ease

Dr. Ease was the busiest man in town. People came from all of the neighboring communities and waited in a long line to see him. The line moved quickly, though, because Dr. Ease was extremely fast in ministering to his patients. He gave them each a pill, depending on their primary symptom. This particular morning his new apprentice looked very worried as he gazed out at the waiting line, which seemed to snake around for miles. Dr. Ease remained calm as ever.

"Doctor," whined the anxious apprentice, "we are out of almost all of the pills." We're down to 10 Fever pills, 8 Pain pills, 7 Diet pills, 4 Diarrhea pills, 3 Phobia pills, 1 Depression pill, and none of all the rest. Except for Constipation pills—we've got tons of those."

"Then what are you fretting about, Ward? We'll give them all Constipation pills."

"But, Doctor, not everybody in that huge line is constipated. People come here with all kinds of problems."

"Don't worry, Ward. Here, take a Constipation pill and I'll tell you my little secret. All of the pills are the same, but you must not tell anyone because they like to think they're different. They don't understand that all of their symptoms are warning signs that their systems are out of balance."

Ward was looking a little constipated now. "What are you saying, Doctor? Fever and pain are physiological symptoms, while overeating and depression are often psychologically induced. How can they all be treated the same way?"

"Ward, fever is a messenger telling us we've been invaded by a foreign substance which has thrown our bodies out of kilter. It says, 'Stay in bed and conserve your energy, which I will use to raise your temperature and kill off the invaders.'"

"What about pain?"

"Pain says, 'This part of your body needs to remain still so it can heal.'"

"What about vomiting and diarrhea?"

"Oh, they are screaming at us, 'You're crazy if you eat anything else. Can't you see your digestive system is out of whack?'"

"But how can one pill eliminate all of those different symptoms?"

"Ward, we don't want to eliminate the symptom. We want to eliminate what stands between us and the message the symptom is trying to bring."

"Wh'what stands between?" Ward asked, not sure he wanted to hear the answer.

"Fear."

"Hmmm, and what about the behavioral and emotional problems? What are they saying to us?"

"Oh, that's how we handle our fear. We try to drown it, or stuff it, or numb it, or run away from it. But it always comes with us."

Now Ward looked a little green and very skeptical. "Doctor, they never taught us anything like this in medical school."

"Of course not, Ward. They're in the business of keeping people alive, not showing them how to enjoy the wondrous gift of life."

Trembling slightly, Ward began, "I'm a bit afraid to ask, Doctor, but what's in this magic pill of yours?"

Why, the antidote for fear, Ward—Gratitude."

"Gratitude!?!"

"Here, take another Constipation pill, Ward, and sit down and think about it for a while. I've got miles of patients to attend to."

Good and Plenty

Becoming more grateful for who I am and what I have at any given moment opened the door for me to experience a more abundant life. Before then, I had no idea of how good and plenty worked together. Now it seems obvious that the more I appreciate the good in my life, the more open I am to receive; and the more plentiful my life becomes, the more grateful I am, and on and on and on.

But this is all fairly new to me. Because my parents were children of the Great Depression and later lived with the rationing of such household staples as sugar, butter and coffee during World War II, they developed what was known as a "Depression mentality" or a belief in scarcity. This would show up in ways like my two role models, Mom and Aunt Sophie, never buying a new dress unless there were at least two weddings and three Bar or Bat Mitzvahs that they could wear it to.

A belief in scarcity often means seeing life as a balance scale, wherein more on one side equates to less on the other. I totally bought into this paradigm because it was my reality. If there were five cookies and my brother Spencer and cousin Stuart each took two, that left only one for me. And, indeed, that is true for material resources; however, I had generalized the concept to include intangibles. So if someone's side of the balance scale was weighted with success or love, for instance, somehow that made my side have less and I felt envious. The scales finally tipped in my favor when I learned to appreciate what's in my life *without regard for what others have.* And I was able to accept abundance without guilt when I understood that my having plenty didn't make someone else's scale any less full.

Also, there's the phenomenon of our ever-changing perceptions. What might seem like success or a good thing, can become not so desirable around the next bend in the road (like Lottery winners finding out the extra money not only didn't make their problems disappear but brought new ones with it). And what might seem like defeat or a bad thing can lead to something even better than the previous situation.

How many times have you heard of someone who lost a job or a close relationship and wound up finding a much better match?

And then there's the memory factor. I used to feel a lack when I would miss out on a social gathering that I was either not invited to or unable to attend. One day some friends and I were reminiscing and someone mentioned a particularly fun-filled occasion that I had not been a part of. Everyone except me eagerly shared their happy memories and at one point, unable to pinpoint a certain detail, they turned to me to see if I remembered. Do you see the significance? Years later, no one remembered that I wasn't there! It didn't matter if I had attended or not. And I got to share their happy memories as if they were my own.

Life, indeed, is good and plentiful, as long as I *expect nothing and appreciate everything.*

Morning Gratitude Prayer

Good morning, Heavenly Family/All That Is.
Thank you for this most miraculous gift of life.

Thank you for this strong, healthy, vital, vibrant,
fit and fabulous mind-body-spirit.
May I take the very best care of her.

Thank you for surrounding me with loving
family and friends. Please bless them all.
May we know the truth of who we are:
the Love, the Beauty, the Peace, the Joy.
May we fully embody our true nature and
lavishly share it with all those we meet.

Thank you for the ever-flowing Cornucopia of Life.
May I be discerning with the wealth of possibilities,
do my best with the ripe opportunities,
and remain an open channel for Divine Inspiration
to come through me and out to the world
in all sorts of creative expressions and loving acts.

And may I receive Life's riches,
both material and ethereal,
with amazing grace and gratitude.

Thank you for the glorious gift of today.
May I live it well.

Finding Her Way

Finding *Your* Way

Before answering the questions, please take a few moments to think or write about what the pieces evoked in you.

Questions

1. What are you currently taking for granted?

2. How can you become familiar with people or situations and maintain your appreciation for them?

3. Think of what you fear most in your life right now. How might a Gratitude pill help?

4. Do you believe more in scarcity or in abundance? What role does gratitude play in that?

5. Do you have a regular gratitude practice? If not, I invite you to write your own prayer of appreciation—or feel free to use mine.

13 Truth & Consequences

The Road to Truth

It isn't always comfortable:
sometimes it's messy,
sometimes it's painful,
sometimes others get hurt.

It knocks down all of my fences:
my defenses,
my offenses,
my on-the-fences.

It forces me to grow or get off:
It challenges me,
it humbles me,
it crumbles the not-me.

It strips me bare:
innocent as a newborn,
open as a blossom,
simple as the naked truth.

Don't Bother Me, I'm Searching for God

Sitting cross-legged in her living room, June arched her back and then, one by one, relaxed all of her muscles. The sweet music and sandalwood incense helped set the mood for her to clear her mind. Behind her closed eyes, the familiar ball of purple light whirled and pulsated to the rhythm of her deep yogic breathing, and she felt at one with the universe. Then, from a distance she heard a strident voice call, "Mimi, oh Mimi," and Mrs. Hatch had once again shattered June's spiritual attunement.

"That damned dog," thought June, "and that damned nuisance of a neighbor, forever doting on a manicured ball of fluff!"

"Junie, honey, have you seen Mimi?"

"Mrs. Hatch, you know I always meditate at this hour. Please don't bother me."

June was determined not to allow Mrs. Hatch's inane mothering of that little creature to interrupt her search for Self. Yet, each day brought another version of the same story. June might be reading a book called *Finding Your God Within,* or some similar title, and be just about to grasp the key concept when her neighbor's shrill voice would ring out, "Oh, Junie, come see how cute Mimi looks in her new sweater."

"Please don't bother me now, Mrs. Hatch," June would implore. "I'm reading something really important." And she would shake her head in amazement at how that lady could fill her life with such trivia.

On the evenings that her spiritual study group met at June's home, Mrs. Hatch always found some excuse to come over and disturb them. "Junie, I need you to polish the fingers on my right hand," or "Junie, I want you to see the new towels I bought," or "Junie, Mimi's not feeling well tonight. What should I do?"

June would invariably take a deep yogic breath and slowly reply, "Please don't bother me now, Mrs. Hatch. I've a very important meeting going on." And the group would praise June for her patience with her annoying neighbor.

Incredibly, the interruptions to June's inner peace went on for many years, during which time she learned four different forms of meditation, made two trips to India, did Sufi dancing and Buddhist chanting, and even tried playing Tibetan bowls. But inevitably her concentration was broken by Mrs. Hatch's insistent calls.

In her retirement years, June gave up her lifelong search, traded in her meditation cushion for a recliner, and became a soap opera addict. Still, Mrs. Hatch's nerve-shattering voice, pandering to her silly mutt (Mimi had been replaced by Claude and then Jacques), pierced her inner peace.

June eventually became a bedridden, bitter old lady who felt that her earnest attempts at finding God had gone completely unrewarded. Her eyesight too weak to watch television, she lay in bed, eyes closed, breathing so shallowly her body barely moved.

One day the dancing purple light returned, then turned to brilliant white, and an outstretched arm emerged. She knew in an instant her maker had come for her. "God," she croaked, "why has it been so hard? Why did you not give me any help?"

"Oh, my dear Junie," rasped the frighteningly familiar voice, "I tried. I certainly tried."

Somebody's Got to Play the Heavy

Sometimes when faced with someone whom I find truly obnoxious, someone whose sole purpose in life seems to be pushing my buttons, I remind myself that this person is doing me the favor of bringing my limitations to light so that I can grow beyond them. In fact, that person is doing all of us a favor by taking on a role few people would want to play. At those times, one of my favorite fantasies pops on my mind-screen, the one about a group of souls divvying up roles prior to coming into their next incarnation.

Celestial Casting

"Okay, everyone, let's see who wants what role."

"Does anyone mind if I play the sweet ingénue this time? It's been centuries since I've done that one."

"I don't care. But I just got through playing the heavy and don't want to do that one again—not for eons."

"Why don't you play the sloppy drunk? You do that one so well."

"What about you, Soul 105892? How about you playing the heavy this time?"

"Oh, no, not me. I'm tired of not being liked. I want to be the high school cheerleader or football hero."

"What about you, Soul 93644, you've had everyman and everywoman roles lately. Would you like to play the heavy?"

"Not me. I'm ready to be a charismatic leader."

"Don't even ask me. I want to be a seductress."

"And I want to be a mild-mannered reporter."

"Come on, everyone, show some team spirit. Somebody's got to play the heavy."

Getting to the Truth

Like June in the story, I tried numerous New Age methods for finding Truth, Self, God. The countless books and lectures and workshops and satsangs and study groups and wise people from various traditions, all seemed to have a similar message—look inside, through numerous techniques (prayer, meditation, silent retreats, tarot cards, recording one's dreams). I found that I did not have much of a propensity for any of those methods. In desperation one day, I implored from the depth of my being, "If you want me to know something, please just tell me or show me in a way that's easy for me to understand."

Something astounding happened. Some consciousness in the universe seemed to have heard my plea and began responding as requested. One day, at a time when I was struggling to make fit yet another relationship that was the wrong size, I was pushing a cart full of groceries across the street when a car that was supposed to stop for pedestrians didn't. I had an instant to react—time only to stop and let go of the cart. The next instant, BAM! The car smashed into the metal cart, sending its contents flying through the air. As I looked at the eggs splattered on the pavement, I was keenly aware that that could have been me down there. An hour later, after I'd stopped shaking, I said, "Okay, that came across loud and clear: I need to let go of the relationship to save myself. Do you think next time you could communicate a little less dramatically?"

In time I learned that when I paid more attention to my intuition, I needed neither dreams nor real-world dramatizations. Still, there seemed to be something missing. The spiritual truths that I had gleaned from all of my studies were not fully incorporated into my daily living. I observed that gap in others' behavior as well. Like June, they might speak eloquently about *how* to live rightly, even quote chapter and verse of whatever ideology they espoused, without actually *living* rightly. I began to understand that what may appear as hypocrisy can merely result from our "getting it" intellectually prior to our *really* getting it. At some point, I got it—to know the Oneness is to experience it in every person and every situation.

It's so simple. I had taken enough workshops and read enough books. It was time for me to start treating others as divine beings— even when they forget who they really are. The problem is, I sometimes forget who *I* really am.

Mommy, Where Did the Sun Go?

One day the sun disappeared. Just like that. It had been there the day before and the day before that, and now it wasn't. Mikey was very concerned. Looking out his bedroom window, he knew Mommy would not let him go outside to play today. She'd say it was too cold and that he'd better stay inside.

Beyond his disappointment, Mikey was curious. There had been days when part of the sun was here and part of it was not, but never like this. Where did it go? Would it come back? Would he be a prisoner inside the house forever?

He ran to his mother with alarm in his voice. "Mommy, Mommy, the sun is all gone!" She laughed quietly and smiled her sweet Mommy smile, "No, honey, it's not gone, just hiding for a while behind those clouds. This would be a good day for you to stay inside and work your new puzzles."

There it was. The verdict had been handed down. The sun decides to go away and Mikey has to stay inside to play. It just wasn't fair! "But, Mommy, how long is it going to hide? Is it playing hide-and-seek? Should I count to 20?"

Mommy put down her dish towel and gave Mikey her full attention. "The sun isn't really hiding, honey. I just said that to be funny." Then she arranged some items on the kitchen table. "Look at the orange, Mikey. Pretend that's the sun. And here comes the salt and pepper shakers. Pretend they are clouds floating by. Do you see how they cover up part of the orange? Now they leave and you can see all of the orange again."

Mikey nodded his head in big up-and-down motions. "But the sun is *all* gone. There's nothing in the sky."

Mommy then moved a box of cereal in front of the orange. "Mikey, can you see the orange now?" Mikey shook his head in big side-to-side motions.

"Where is it?" Mommy asked.

Grinning from ear to ear, Mikey grabbed the orange from in back of the cereal box. "Here it is!" he proudly proclaimed, holding up the orange for Mommy to see.

"Where was it before you took it?" she asked.

"There," he pointed in back of the box.

"Did the orange go away?"

"No," Mikey giggled. "The orange can't walk!"

"Why couldn't you see it?" asked Mommy.

"Because the *Krispy Oats* were hiding it."

"Well," said Mommy, "that's what has happened to the sun today, Mikey. You can't see it because the clouds are in front of it, but it's still there. It's always there, whether you can see it or not."

"When will the clouds go away, Mommy?"

"Oh," she pondered, "when they're good and ready."

The Simple Truth

Uncomfortable feelings seem to come upon us from out of nowhere. They plague us for a couple of minutes, or hours, or days—sometimes for years. Life can be pretty bleak during those times when our sunny nature is blotted out by painful emotions or dark moods. When that happens to me I am truly stuck inside, playing in my head with thoughts that hold the darkness in place.

Sometimes it seems like the sun, my natural, nurturing inner light, has been extinguished for good. No more joy, only hollow laughter and fake smiles. Like Mikey, I wonder, "Where did the love and my *joie de vivre* go? They were here yesterday and the day before."

I've gone down more black roads than I choose to remember. Faith is a traveling companion that was a long time coming. Not faith in a god or a religion, but faith that what is real—my loving, beautiful spirit—will always be real. Crushing events come and go. Despairing thoughts come and go. Even yearnings, so strong I fear my heart will burst if they're not met, come and go. Everything comes and goes except the truth of who I really am.

Who are *you,* really?

The Beautiful White Rabbit

Last week a marvelous magician came to town with a traveling show. He pulled out vibrant-colored scarves and juggled balls with perfect balance and grace. But most enchanting of all was the bunny, the beautiful white bunny he pulled out of his hat. He let me play with the bunny for several days. The bunny hopped this way and that, he snuggled up to me and licked my fingers. As we played and loved, the bunny grew larger each day, until he became a magnificent, full-grown rabbit.

On the fifth night, as the show was preparing to leave, the magician came to me and said, "Don't cry because the rabbit's leaving. He wasn't real to begin with. Look, there's nothing in the hat."

I looked, and he was right. The rabbit had vanished. Could it be that there had never been a beautiful white bunny? That it was all a trick? Just a vision of what I wanted to be real?

I looked at the magician and said, "No, the rabbit was here for five days. I saw him, I felt him, I loved him. Maybe *you* don't believe he's real, but I know he is. And it doesn't matter if I never see him again because I have met him and he will always be real for me."

The magician looked confused as he tipped over the hat again, as if he wanted to believe the rabbit was still around but couldn't see him.

I watched the traveling show ride out of town the following day, but I didn't see the magician. I headed home through a wooded area and right there, in the center of the path, was the rabbit, radiating his magnificence. Oh, I hugged him, and we danced and played.

"Where's the magician?" I asked.

"There's no magician," he said. "He was only a vision of what you were afraid was real."

Finding *Your* Way

Before answering the questions, please take a few moments to think or write about what the pieces evoked in you.

Questions

1. Describe your inner Beautiful White Rabbit and your outer Magician.

2. What do you do when you see yourself being less than who you know you're capable of being?

3. Which personality types or "heavies" do you have the most trouble dealing with? Can you see the positive role they play in your life?

4. Do you have a way of seeing beneath another's façade to their more glorious inner self?

5. What important truths about life has your journey brought you?

14. Living Consciously

What Are You Not Seeing?

Children teach us to see. For instance, the first time we took my grandson Ryan to the zoo, my daughter Robin and I looked at the animals. We kept pointing and excitedly saying, "Ryan, do you know what animal that is?" or "Look at that monkey, Ryan" and "Ryan, do you see that tall giraffe?" Despite our gestures, enthusiasm, and, yes, pleading, Ryan said nothing.

As I mentioned, Robin and I were looking at the animals. Ryan, being in a stroller, about two feet off the ground, was looking at other things that he found fascinating, like people's legs, twigs and stones, and Robin and me frantically gesturing. We must have looked pretty funny to him.

That outing showed me how out of touch I was with a child's perspective, but I didn't truly appreciate the wonder of a child's view until I took Ryan to my neighborhood park.

Prince Ryan and the Magic Chip

At the playground, three-year-old Ryan declined my invitation to push him on the swing and bypassed the multicolored, state-of-the-art equipment, to play instead with the wood chips that were often trampled upon and all but invisible to the adults.

First grinning and saying "Whee!" as he threw them in the air, then tirelessly making trip after trip, using little boy handfuls to move them from the play area to the cement, Ryan finally struck gold. His eyes glinted with glee as he spied the ultimate wood chip. About the size of a small domino, it was more of a chunk than a chip. But to Ryan, it was a treasure—the Hope Diamond would have been tossed aside for it.

He toted the chip here and there, pushed it through slats in the benches, flung it this way and that, but leave it? Never! It came home with us. And was it magical? Most definitely—it opened my eyes to unseen possibilities. Ryan's had never closed.

It's All About Consciousness

Many people think I'm nice or kind or even a good person. I don't. Somewhere along the way I started moving into a different conceptual paradigm. You know the one most of us grow up with. It's based on evaluating people, things, behavior, moods, situations—just about everything—according to how they compare to what we think they should be. That makes things good or bad, right or wrong, wonderful or horrible, kind or mean, according to where they fall on the barometer of "shouldness."

The paradigm I operate within more and more of the time, now, is based on degrees of consciousness. Like the aperture of a camera, our consciousness can be narrow or wide, depending on whether we want to focus in or out on something. For instance, you're walking up to the entrance of a building and there's another person nearby who's holding a big box that requires both hands. Do you open the door for the other person? Of course. Well, most of the time. There are other times when your consciousness has narrowed its focus on something like a loved one who's ill or a sales presentation you will be pitching. You are temporarily so self-absorbed that your focus is limited to a narrow passageway from you to the building. You open the door and let it slam shut after you because you didn't see the other person with the large bundle—not because you suddenly became an old meanie.

Similarly, the person carrying the bundle will see you as being rude, unkind, or even an asshole, depending on the narrowness of *their* focus at the time, and will make no judgment at all if their consciousness is expanded enough to realize that you must have something on your mind that is making you unaware of their needing some assistance with the door.

Then there are the times when people see the person with the bundle and still do not hold the door open for them. We can call that person malicious, sociopathic, depressed, or simply unaware. It's all a matter of how conscious we are at that moment.

Being Present with Presence in the Present

In one book after another (and possibly even before there were books), the virtues of living in the moment have been extolled, explained, and exemplified. There's nothing left for us to do but to do it. Except if you've sincerely tried to remain present in the moment, you've likely found, as have I, that it is quite a daunting challenge. To simply will myself to stop thinking has not been possible. I immediately start thinking about the pain in my left shoulder, or what's next on my day's agenda, or how difficult it is to stop thinking.

I wish I could tell you that I've made wonderful progress in staying *present* (fully focused on what's happening) with *presence* (coming from my true nature) in the *present* (with no thoughts or feelings about my past or future); but it has been a monumental undertaking for me, given my active imagination. Whatever progress I've made in being more present amounts to finding ways of reminding myself to refocus on the now instead of mentally or emotionally being somewhere else.

Here is my latest technique: When I'm aware of not being present (usually because I'm not happy), I say to myself, "This is my entire life right now." I know, there's nothing particularly profound about that phrase, but for some reason it works for me—for now. When I use this phrase, shift happens.

I'm chomping at the bit waiting for the traffic light to turn green. "Sydney, this is your entire life right now." [Big breath] I'm sitting comfortably in my car listening to beautiful music on the radio, often amused at the antics of the other drivers and the pedestrians.

I'm pushing myself to cook dinner rather than eat out of a can. "Sydney, this is your entire life right now." [Big breath] I'm enjoying the feel of the carrot as I peel it and the near-ecstasy-producing smell of fresh garlic and basil, while sipping wine and listening to a mellow CD.

Finding Her Way

I'm tossing and turning, trying to get back to sleep after being awakened by apartment noises, worrying about tomorrow's whatever. "Sydney, this is your entire life right now." [Big breath] I'm cozily snuggling under the covers, listening to my neighbors make love or war, or to birdies singing their good mornings.

I'm thinking about what I want to say when the person across from me finally finishes their long-winded discourse of what I could have said in two short sentences. "Sydney, this is your entire life right now." [Big breath] I'm feeling a loving connection to whomever, listening to their whatever with genuine interest because <u>this whomever and whatever are my entire life right now</u>.

I have no greater wisdom to impart on the subject of remaining present in the moment. Most often it still eludes me. Yet, I will keep on that road because that's where my life is.

Love *Is* the Thing

Earlier in this book, I mentioned learning some truths about love: that it lasts as long as it lasts and that it can never be destroyed. Understanding the third part, about love being neither created nor gotten from someone else, was a long time coming; but that piece turned out to be such a gem for me that it was worth the wait—and then some.

The Spigot People

Once upon a time in a faraway land, lived a group of people who had spigots attached to their hearts. Whenever their spigots were open, love flowed through their bodies and out to others, as well, through their smiles and their touch. As long as everyone kept their spigots open, they were filled with love all of the time.

But because the Spigot People (also called "Spigoteers") didn't understand the mechanics of how their spigots worked and didn't know whose love-flow was filling whom, they would sometimes make themselves miserable. If someone were having a stressful day, for instance, and inadvertently shut off their spigot, that person might accuse another Spigoteer, "You haven't been giving me enough love lately. You must have closed your spigot."

Bewildered, the second Spigoteer would respond, "No, I didn't close mine, it's been open all day. It's *your* spigot that's closed."

"Well, you made mine close when you aimed your love-flow at other people."

"But I never turned off my love for *you*; it can flow in more than one direction."

"No, it can't, else I would be happy."

And sometimes when the Spigot People were feeling really good, they would think, "I want to keep this love right here. I don't want to lose it." So they would close their spigots to stop the flow; but the love they wanted to hold onto would seep out of their fingers and hair and dribble down onto the ground, and eventually they would feel no love at all. Then they would complain, "How come nobody loves me? I must be too ugly, or too old, or too unlucky."

The Spigot People were very lucky, however, that a plumber happened to be passing through Spigotville and noticed that the Spigoteers had no idea that they controlled the degree to which they were filled with love. So he took an ordinary garden hose, connected it to a water spigot, and showed the townspeople that as long as the spigot was open, the hose remained inflated with water and when the spigot was closed, the hose collapsed. Next, he took a second hose and aimed its spray at the first one. He aimed it at the middle and he aimed it at the nozzle; but wherever he aimed it, the hose on the ground remained flat because the flow from the other hose could not fill it up.

"You're so lucky, Spigot People, because just like this hose and the water, all you have to do is keep your *own* spigot open in order to be filled with love. Now, others' love certainly feels good when its spray touches you, but it's the love from your own spigot that fills and expands you."

Excited whispers rustled through the group, and one puzzled-looking Spigoteer stepped forward. "But if other Spigoteers can't turn on my love-flow," he said, "they can't turn it off, either."

"Right," beamed the plumber.

"Well, then what turns it off?"

The whispering stopped as silent Spigoteers stared at the plumber scratching his head. "As near as I can figure out" he finally said, "your love-flow stops when you try to mind someone else's spigot instead of your own."

What's It All About?

When I was 12 years old, I lost faith in organized religion. Science was the ideology we were taught in public school, and there was not much that was logical or empirical about what we were told in Sunday school. It was another 20 years before I encountered the notion of spirituality that was not connected to religion. It transformed my life. I now knew how to make things meaningful. I now had a community of like-minded thinkers. I now had direction.

My beliefs have continued to change over the years, becoming progressively simpler. I believe in love. I believe in being kind and generous merely for the echo of it. I believe that like attracts like, which is a great motivator for being kind and generous. I believe in the immense power of being fully present with an open heart and mind. I believe there is one life force in the universe of which we are all an expression. I believe that as our consciousness expands, life gets continually simpler.

Beyond that, I know very little. My 12-year-old's questions about the purpose of life, in general, and my specific purpose for being here are still without answers. But my frustration with not knowing has been replaced, more and more, with an awe-filled delight for the mystery and the magic that we call life.

I hope that as you validate your unique experiences, you will cherish them as your Goldilocks way of finding out what's right for you. Of course, what's right is only for that moment. We never know what adventure lurks around Serendipity's next bend that could change right-fit to misfit or best fit of all.

She Awoke

She awoke, cringing at her mother's cheerful "Good morning!", sick to her stomach at the thought of another day of sitting in class, half hearing the teacher's voice drone through her recycled lessons, half hearing the children outside, laughing on the playground.

ح

She awoke, cringing at the digital clock's fluorescent announcement that it was time to get up and spend another day sitting in meetings, half hearing middle managers pitching their recycled strategies, half hearing the staff next door, chatting in the lunchroom.

ح

She awoke, in the middle of the night, enjoying an entire minute before her body remembered it was supposed to be aching, half hearing the inner noise of yesterday's recycled events, half hearing the outside noise that had disturbed her sleep.

ح

She awoke, lusciously lolling in bed, every cell in her body grateful to be almost pain free and in relatively good working order, half aware of the sun seeping through the window shades, fully aware of the precious gift she'd been given—another day.

ح

She awoke.

Finding *Your* Way

Before answering the questions, please take a few moments to think or write about what the pieces evoked in you.

Questions

1. What would your average day be like if you lived it with the wonder of a small child?

2. Can you imagine an entirely different paradigm for life, one based on consciousness rather than expectations, comparisons, and shoulds?

3. What do you do to stay present in the moment?

4. If no one can give you love or take it away, what causes your love spigot to open and close?

5. Have you had any awakening experiences, where you were totally present and at peace with the world exactly as it is?

Epilogue

When I'd finished reading the poem, "Growling Tiger, Crouching Little Girl" to the training group on our second weekend of the program, there was not a sound in the room except for the sniffles of a couple of women. I slowly looked around the circle, meeting the eyes of each person. It was unbelievably empowering to appear so emotionally naked in front of them. One man, to whom I had felt especially invisible the previous month, held my eyes for a moment, then nodded and said, "I see you. I hear you." It meant so much to me. Thank you, Rick.

And for you, the reader, I wish that you will be seen and heard, perhaps by a friend with whom you share your experiences, perhaps by a group of which you are a part. Hopefully, by the one who matters the most—you. It can be an exhilarating experience to read what you've written aloud, to hear the sound of your words, even when alone.

Better fly, Butterfly,
now is the time.

Acknowledgements

A heartfelt thanks is given

To Jan Frances for planting the outrageous seed of writing a book about my life. To Co-Directors Rosie Kuhn and Todd Zimmerman and the members of the 2006-2007 Transformational Life Coaching group, who provided the incubator for that seed.

To Jim Fadiman, author and teacher, for encouraging me to fictionalize my writing. To John Axtell, Emily Hallowell, and Cynthia Ng for bringing the writings into full color and beauty.

To my manuscript readers and friends Christine Brooks, Joan Gielow, Dana Kavy, and Roslyn Moore, whose feedback helped to keep the book both readable and meaningful.

To the Monday Women's Group in Naas, Ireland, of which me daughter Beth is a member, for being the first group to try out the study questions and help bring my vision into reality.

To the staff, faculty and students at the Institute of Transpersonal Psychology, who nurture me on a daily basis. And to my loving friends and family who have sustained me on my journey in so many ways, mainly by believing in my ability to thrive wherever the journey takes me.

To the book's endorsers, Judy Grahn, Shiloh Sophia McCloud, Bruce Moore and Denise Roy, whose kind words on the back cover remind me of what a joy it was to be able to write this book.

An extra special thanks to Margaret Hartwell, friend and coach extraordinaire, for supporting me through the writing and publication of my first-born book and whose input has been invaluable. Margaret can be contacted at www.liveworkcoaching.org. And to my buddies Cyd Percin and Marsha Tucker, my unofficial coaches in everything.

Dear Reader

If you have been touched by this book, I invite you to use the contact information listed below. I would love to hear from you.

About the Author

Sydney J. Reuben has taught, coached, and presented workshops on self-esteem and empowerment for over 25 years. Her current focus is on helping others find their unique way of being in the world. She is also an administrator at the Institute of Transpersonal Psychology in Palo Alto, California.

To contact Sydney, please email her at Sydney@sydneyjreuben.com. To learn more about *Finding Her Way* study groups, weekend workshops or individual coaching, please visit www.sydneyjreuben.com.

Share *Finding Her Way* with a Friend

Website Orders: sydneyjreuben.com

Postal Orders: Growling Tiger Publishing, P.O. Box 50516,
Palo Alto, CA 94303-0516

For one or two friends: ___ copies @ $17.00 each

For 3 or more friends: ___ copies @ $15.00 each

For signed copies, list the first name of each friend:

_____

_____

___ Include a free copy of *"Finding Her Way* Study Group Guidelines."

Ship-to Name _____
Address _____
City _____
State _____ Zip _____
Telephone _____
Email Address _____

Sales Tax: If shipped to a California address, add 8.25% for sales tax.
U.S. Shipping: $4.00 for first book and $2.00 for each additional copy.
International Shipping: Inquire at Sydney@sydneyjreuben.com.

___ Enclosed is a check for $ _____ (includes shipping).

___ Please charge my Credit Card $ _____ (includes shipping).

Name on Card _____ Exp. Date _____
Card No. _____ Sec. Code _____
Card Owner's Address (if different from above):

_____

_____

Thank you for your generous order. 10% of the gross profits will be donated
to the **Seva Foundation Fund for Women & Girls**, empowering women
worldwide (www.seva.org).

Printed in the United States
150250LV00001B/2/P

9 780615 271330